BEATING ANXIETY AND DEPRESSION FOR LIFE

Printed in the United States of America
First Printing, 2018

ISBN: 978-1717597694

Printed by Homestead Books: Starkville, Mississippi
www.thehomesteadcenter.com

Book design by Michelle M. White
www.mmwgraphicdesign.com

Beating Anxiety & Depression
for Life

*Brain and Body
Techniques
that Work*

ALISON BUEHLER, EdD
BUDDY WAGNER, PhD
LYNN PETERSON, MS, LPC

Table of Contents

Preface

There is a major shift happening in our understanding of mental illness and mood disorders. As our insight into how the brain functions improves, we discard old theories and replace them with new ones. For years, we believed that the secret to mental health was balanced brain chemistry. We know now that brain, body, environment, and even our beliefs are all interconnected, interdependent, and share a secret language we are beginning to translate. Armed with this new wisdom, we are making huge leaps in mental health treatment. As Dr. Kelly Brogan demonstrates so clearly in her book, *A Mind of Your Own*, depression and anxiety are not simply serotonin deficiencies. They are the body's alarm system telling you "something is wrong!" Depression and anxiety, as all-encompassing as they feel, are simply *symptoms* of an underlying imbalance. And, you can address the things that cause the alarm system to sound.

I wouldn't have believed that ten years ago. I bought fully into the notion that my body or brain just did not work right, and I believed it would take a lifetime of pharmaceuticals to cause them to function correctly. In fact, a woman who presented at a wellness conference enraged me when she described how she experienced a psychotic break and slowly pulled herself into a state of un-medicated, fully functional happiness through diet, self-compassion, and embracing the darkness. That really made me angry because I believed it was not possible for me. I was wrong.

After two decades of war with my albatross, I decided I was sick of being "sick." Do you ever feel that way? I had had it with a medication that made me ill if I missed a dose, was fed up with a half-life feeling, and was tired of being tired. Even though that darkness terrified me, I was ready to take a chance. I dug in deep and leaped in, held on by my fingernails, and prayed. I read and read and read, went to workshops, did lots of yoga, started meditating, and took a million supplements. And I sunk like a rock. But this time something was different. I knew it wouldn't kill me. I knew I couldn't die because of my three children. I stayed with it. And slowly, like a frog blinking its eyes under the mud in spring, I crawled out. What I found blew my best expectations out of the water. For the first time since pre-adolescence, I was well.

For the most part, I am well to this day. My wellness depends on my practice. You cannot expect to keep muscles when you quit working out at the gym. Sometimes I forget. Sometimes I start feeling "normal" for so long that I let things slide. It doesn't take long to land back in the mud. But, the mud doesn't scare me like it used to. It may feel rotten. I may get a panic here and there, like, "I'll suffocate!" or "I cannot stand one more second in this body!" But, my body and mind are learning to trust the process. Sinking and rising are just part of the natural cycle of life. I told my mom recently, "Now, I just blow 'normal' a kiss as I swing by it on the way up or down."

The Nobel Prize winning monk, Thich Nhat Hanh, sums this journey up beautifully saying, "Most people are afraid of suffering. But suffering is a kind of mud to help the lotus flower of happiness grow. There can be no lotus flower without the mud. There is plenty of mud in the world."

My security lies in the fact that I now possess the tools to move through both, as I call them, "the mean reds" and "the rainbow periods," which is why I wanted to write this book. It is possible to find good information on healing the body and brain from anxiety and depression, but it isn't easy. We are a quick-fix, disease/treatment culture and wellness takes hard work. If you are ready to dig in and learn to move through the mud to dry ground, this book is for you. I enlisted two of the most qualified people I have encountered along my journey to help give you the tools to make your own pilgrimage.

Buddy Wagner is a modern-day magician. In reality, he is a Baptist minister turned national board-certified counselor and clinical hypnotherapist, but I have seen him work magic. What I call magic, he calls science mixed with faith. Buddy studied theology, but says he gave it up for sex when he dropped out of seminary to get married. He was kidding, of course, but this light-hearted, almost playful personality that Buddy brings to the usually serious realm of mental health is refreshing. Buddy became a counselor and sees clients in private practice part-time, while teaching in the Counseling Education Department at Mississippi College.

I met Buddy when he presented at a workshop called *The Mind-Body Connection*. The workshop was designed to teach counselors the latest, most effective methods of treating clients and was based on the groundbreaking work coming out on brain imaging. The organizer was a counselor at my child's school, and she asked if she could rent our retreat center to host the event. I jumped at the opportunity, largely because I was intrigued by the topic and wanted to attend as a non-counselor. I had been reading about neuroplasticity and the new techniques for dealing with depression emerging out of this research. Having achieved some relief from my own depression by changing the way I ate made me hopeful, but I still had a long way to go.

Buddy is a physically small man, but you forget that as soon as he starts talking. His influence and charisma fill a room. Buddy's calm presence and enthusiastic voice drew the audience in immediately. He began by saying, "I don't think talk therapy is a very cost or time-efficient model. In my early days as a therapist, I would see clients who had been in therapy for years and were still drudging over the same issues from childhood. I began to dread those clients, and I thought, 'There must be a better way.'"

The better way Buddy found remarkably improved outcomes for his clients. He told us his work involved actually retraining the brain and that he had seen it happen fairly quickly and consistently with clients. I was skeptical. I believed I had been born with a brain that didn't fire correctly and, at best, hoped to learn how to manage this faulty wiring effectively. Buddy piqued my curiosity. Could this be true? Without surgery or medicine, was it possible to actually rewire the brain?

Before teaching a few of his favorite techniques Buddy said, "If I can't help someone in three or four sessions, I can't help them." That statement flew in the face of everything I had ever heard about counseling. Didn't it take years to undo a lifetime of habits and thought patterns? According to Buddy Wagner's experiences, the exciting answer was, "No."

The practice of "brain rewiring" is only one of the new understandings turning mental health treatment, as it has been practiced for almost one-hundred-years, on its head. Even those of us who are not in counseling or human sciences are beginning to hear a lot about neuropathways and how they develop. An experienced counselor at the workshop explained to me, "Neuropathways are like a riverbed that forms after years and years of water flowing toward a lower point and around obstacles. A well-worn-groove forms in our brains, but some of these pathways are unhelpful. You can actually train your brain to jump out of the worn riverbed and create a new one that is more beneficial for this period in your life." Scientists call this ability to reshape the brain "neuroplasticity." *Psychology Today* describes neuroplasticity in an article by Dr. Constance Scharff saying, "We used to think that the brain, once damaged, could not repair itself. Breakthroughs in neuroscience have shown that this is not true. Though individual neurons might be damaged beyond repair, the brain attempts to heal itself when damaged by making new connections, or new neural pathways, as work-arounds for the damage. This is called neuroplasticity, neuro (brain/nerve/neuron) and plasticity (mold ability)." This information blew my mind. Could I rewire my brain around my depression? I gobbled up Buddy's techniques and put them into practice.

Then there was Lynn. She was a friend of mine from early motherhood. In all honesty, she was one I avoided because I felt she was quite negative, and I had had all the negativity I could handle from my own brain. Over a decade, I watched curiously as she made the hard choices to end a financially secure marriage, return to school—broke and in the throes of raising two kids—to become a counselor, and transform herself into one of the most vibrant women I've ever met. Now, I watch with amazement as Lynn Peterson leads groups. If you only met her briefly, you would never guess that her soft, humble demeanor changes lives on a regular basis. Lynn is quirky and laughs at herself easily. Maybe these characteristics make her non-threatening enough to reach people. Maybe her undaunted self-journey, which she shares openly, gives people hope. Maybe her unquenchable search for new and better ways to help clients leads her to the most effective practices. Whatever the case, I love watching Lynn work.

In our last workshop together, Lynn asked participants to take out a piece of paper and write down three things they were currently most upset with themselves about. She asked them to choose one issue on the list, sink into their bodies, and find how feelings about this issue were affecting them. Upset stomachs, headaches, tight necks, and agitation all surfaced in response to her probing. She asked her participants to close their eyes and step outside their bodies. "Picture yourself as someone you really care about. It could be a child, a good friend, or a family member.

Imagine they tell you they have this same issue. Now open your eyes and write down what you would say to them."

Lynn has studied doggedly for her practice and for her own life. She introduced me to several very important pieces of mental health, including self-compassion and the mind-body connection. These were my missing pieces.

Buddy and Lynn agreed to help write this book in order to give you the tools you need to transform your life. Don't go back to sleep. Jump in and begin to practice. The shifts may be subtle at first, but stick with it. You can be well. You can feel the full spectrum of human emotions, even the toughest, without dying. And you can be fully alert, awake, and alive.

Alison Buehler

Alison Buehler (signature)

*Dr. Kelly Brogan, M.D. in *A Mind of Your Own,* has done the extensive research on which this book rests. We will not rehash the "case" for using alternative approaches to pharmaceuticals in this book. Pharmaceuticals are appropriate for some people at certain times, but they are not the subject of this book. This is a complementary or supplemental toolkit that helps you find avenues to address root causes of anxiety and depression.

Acknowledgments

This project was a team effort among the authors and a group of readers. We wanted to make the book and workbook as relevant and useful as possible. Our readers helped us shape this into the most helpful toolbox for healing we could imagine. Thank you to Cheryl Conlee, Fay Fisher, Shannon Voges Haupt, Sakina Williams, and Debra Wolf. We couldn't have done this without your insightful contributions.

Introduction

This is a book about healing yourself of depression and/or anxiety. It is not an academic treatment of the subject with an abundance of footnotes; rather, it is a down to earth, how-to book. The medical model has convinced us that drugs are the answer. However, we, the authors, believe there are safer, healthier, more effective ways to heal. This doesn't mean that if you follow what is written in the following pages, depression or anxiety will never occur in your life again. Sometimes depression is appropriate. If you lose a significant relationship, job, or possession, it is healthy to feel depressed, but the depression should not become chronic. It should not last from now until "death do us part." If you are facing a threatening situation or an uncertain situation, you should feel anxious. It is healthy and can assist you in making wise decisions. However, the anxiety should not be so intense that it hinders you from functioning in a healthy way.

We have chosen to describe in this book the tools that we have seen work for clients. You can put some of them to work in your own life today. Others require help from professionally trained practitioners. We created a workbook to go along with this book to guide you through the techniques if you would like further guidance. We want to note that we believe that there are times when medication is an appropriate intervention. You can use these tools alongside medication or alternatively. Weaning off of medication can be very difficult for some people. Please do so under the care of a physician. It is always important to have a supportive family member or friend who is aware of your emotional status. Don't go this alone! Enlist a caring, somewhat objective, partner to let you know how they think you are doing.

Perhaps we should begin by giving definitions of the terms, depression and anxiety, as they are used in the following pages. Depression is a state of feeling sad that influences how one thinks, feels (physically and emotionally), and the way one eats, sleeps and acts. Some think of it as a medical illness or mood disorder that is treatable with drugs; however, this book takes a different approach. Anxiety is a feeling of worry, nervousness, or unease that affects how one thinks and behaves. Some think of it as a disorder that is treatable with drugs. As with depression, this book takes a different approach. We believe that these conditions can be addressed and healed through a combination of providing the body with the nutrition it needs to function optimally, getting enough exercise and sleep, developing our spiritual selves, changing how we think and behave, resolving past traumas, learning to embrace the dark times, and accepting the gifts that depression and anxiety can give us.

While antidepressants are the number one prescribed medication in the country (as many as one in five adults are using them), we don't see their golden promises being fulfilled. In fact, in many cases, antidepressants are barely more effective than placebos, yet our entire mental healthcare system has embraced them as the standard treatment. While these medications are certainly an appropriate treatment in some cases, they don't end depression, anxiety, or any of the other dozens of health issues they are prescribed to treat. They may temporarily put a Band-Aid on the problem, but they do not address the root causes. Antidepressants cannot cure these conditions. However, these underlying conditions can be addressed and you can achieve a quality of life you've been dreaming of.

In this book, we will explore the most common factors underlying anxiety and depression as witnessed in our clients and ourselves. The chemical imbalance model has been reframed by experts like Kelly Brogan, M. D., who demonstrates that depression and anxiety are not serotonin deficiencies. You may need to stop reading here and do some research. Our brains believe what we tell them. If you have spent years believing, as we did, that a chemical imbalance is solely responsible for your condition, you may need to look at the latest evidence. While the chemical imbalance theory gave many of us relief because it implied we did not "cause" our anxiety or depression, holding onto old theories may hinder our progress. We do not believe people cause their depression and anxiety, but we know there are practices and techniques people can put into place to reduce and even eliminate the hold these conditions have on their lives.

Based on new evidence, we believe depression and anxiety are our bodies' alarm systems alerting us to the fact that something important needs attention. You can choose to address these conditions from any of the approaches we introduce and discover what works best for you. Some people prefer to take a more concrete, physical approach, like changing their diet. Others are attracted to retraining their brain and thought patterns. Other people prefer a more metaphysical or spiritual approach to healing. In our experience, making a small change in one part of your system can impact your entire system.

The most important piece of any of these approaches may be how we view our conditions. We must begin by dispelling the belief that we are doomed to be depressed or anxious because our mind or body is faulty. You can be well. Read that again. You can be well! Our understanding of mental health is changing as we are discovering that we can influence our genes, rewire our brains, move trauma through and out of our bodies, and feed our cells in a way that will allow them to function as they were created to function.

The format of the following chapters will be to discuss one of the lenses utilized in the healing process, sharing a story of an individual utilizing this approach successfully, and then giving the reader techniques that can be used to heal. The chapters will be brief and to the point. We do not intend to include fluff to make the book lengthier. We want to give you a book that is easily readable with techniques you can put into practice in a relatively short time. Happy reading!

Chapter 1
Neuro-Linguistic Programming and Other Strategies

We are going to start by sharing our "quick fixes," the practices that we believe provide fast, effective relief. These techniques give you something you can do immediately, at no cost, and in the midst of depressed or anxious feelings. neuro-linguistic programming, positive psychology, mindfulness, and energy psychology are all easy to put into practice in your daily lives. These are well-researched therapies that deliver change quickly.

Neuro-Linguistic Programming (NLP), developed by Richard Bandler and John Grinder, is a powerful way to control and/or change thought patterns, behaviors, and communication patterns. Buddy has discovered through his private practice that NLP techniques can be used to create immediate changes in people that endure over time. He has witnessed clients ridding themselves of phobias, panic attacks, chronic pain, and trauma in powerful ways. Later in this chapter, he will give you examples and explain how you can use NLP to transform your chronic depression or anxiety.

Positive Psychology, first advocated by Martin Seligman, Mihaly Csikszentmihalyi and Christopher Peterson, focuses on values, strengths, virtues, and talents. Buddy finds Positive Psychology to be especially useful with people who are depressed. Later in this chapter, he will present an example and explain how you can use Positive Psychology to alleviate chronic depression.

Mindfulness, introduced to the U.S. medical community by John Kabat-Zinn through his Center for Stress Reduction at the University of Massachusetts, enhances one's attention. It helps you focus on the thoughts, feelings, and physical sensations of the depression or anxiety. Through this process of attention, you become a more objective witness to what's happening and learn to cooperate with the depression or anxiety instead of fighting it or trying to get rid of it. Later in this chapter, Buddy will give you an example and explain how you can use Mindfulness to address chronic depression or anxiety.

Energy Psychology, first popularized by Gary Craig, has developed the Emotional Freedom technique. It is based on acupressure and is done without needles. Instead, you use your fingers to tap certain pressure points on the body. The idea is that emotional or physical pain is caused by energy blockage in the body and the tapping eliminates these blockages so that the energy can flow freely. When this occurs, the pain dissipates.

The beauty of these approaches is that there are no side effects, and you can use them in conjunction with each other. One method may be more effective for you than another, and like anything else, one or some combination will work best for one person, and a different one or combination will work best for someone else. We challenge you to experiment with them to learn which one or combination works best for you. The following stories come directly from Buddy's practice and illustrate how each method can be used to mitigate anxiety and/or depression.

The One-session Remedy

Fran was a twenty-year-old college student who came to see me because of anxiety and panic attacks. She reported that she had had her first panic attack when she was seven and had experienced three to four a week since. She reported constant restlessness and the urge to pick at her skin to the point of developing sores. As we talked, she reported that her anxiety was a nine on a ten-point scale. I then asked Fran to pay attention to her anxiety and tell me what she was experiencing. She mentioned seeing a picture in her mind of an experience that caused her to feel anxious. I asked her to describe the picture. Was it in color or black and white? Was it moving or a still snapshot? What size was it? Where was it located? She described a colorful, moving picture that was life-sized and only a few inches in front of her face.

I then asked Fran to create a picture of a different situation, a situation when she felt calm and to describe the sub-modalities of this picture. This one was still in color, an eight-by-ten snapshot, about ten feet away, down, and to her left. Then, I asked her to see the two pictures side-by-side and gradually move the anxious picture to the location of the calm picture, change it to a still snapshot, and to shrink it to an eight-by-ten. She was able to do this with relative ease. Then, I asked her to repeat this act five times as fast as she could. After each time, she was to imagine a white screen, then the two pictures, then move and change the anxious picture. After this exercise, her anxiety dropped to a two. She was instructed to do this exercise five times a day for the next week. When she returned a week later, she reported that she had had no panic attacks, her red splotches were gone, and the sores on her arms were healing. Fran had created new neural pathways in her brain so that she saw the new powerless picture instead of the powerful one that had been creating the anxiety.

Fran and I could have accomplished the same outcome by exploring which of the characteristics of the anxious picture made it so powerful. I would have had her change the picture from color to black and white to see if the picture was less powerful. Then, she would change it from a moving picture to a still snapshot to see if this made it less powerful. Then, I would have had her shrink it from life size to a smaller size to see if this made it less powerful. And finally, she would move it away from her face to a more comfortable position. When we learned which of these changes took the power away from the picture, I would have asked her to see the original picture and then make the change(s) that took its power away. She would have had to do this act five times, seeing a white screen between each time.

Performance Anxiety

Chris was required to sing in front of his voice class but had been unable to accomplish this due to performance anxiety. When Chris came to see me, he was despondent, convinced that he would never be able to accomplish this requirement. When describing what happened when he experienced the performance anxiety, he mentioned that he saw himself in the 11th grade when he had had to give a speech in class, and some of his classmates made fun of him. He also mentioned that he was in the band in high school and always felt confident and accepted by his band friends. I suggested that we create a very specific mental audio/video of him singing successfully in front of the class with his high school band members around him providing him support. Once the mental video was created, I asked Chris to play it in his mind and tell me what was happening. I asked him to play it three times, and he reported that each time, he felt a little more comfortable. His homework was to practice it throughout the next week. When he returned, he felt more confident but feared that he would freeze up in the actual event.

We tweaked the video to have Chris think that he was going to freeze up prior to singing, but he would focus on his band members and the words they were speaking to him, and this would give him the confidence he needed. This seemed to help with his fear. I saw Chris four times before the scheduled performance. In our fourth meeting, he reported that his confidence was at a 10 and that he had realized that it would be more embarrassing to freeze up than to sing. We met the morning of his performance, and he was still very confident. When we met the next day, Chris reported that he had been successful. He was successful because he created a realistic picture of success, and by viewing it over and over and connecting it to his band experience in high school, he was able to exchange the feelings created by the speech experience with the feelings created by the band experience.

Changing the Voice

When Pat came to see me, he was obviously depressed. His hair was dirty; he was slouched and had no energy. Pat had suffered from depression for several years, which began when he was in a relationship with a woman who constantly degraded him. Prior to this relationship, he had had good self-esteem and was happy; since the relationship, he had been depressed and had low self-esteem. He still heard the voice of his ex-girlfriend putting him down. I asked Pat where he heard the voice. Was it inside his head, behind him, in front of him, etc.? He said it was inside his head. I asked him to let it drift out of his right ear and off into the distance. He was able to do this. When it was off in the distance, I asked him to turn the volume down so that he could barely hear it. He did this. Then I asked him who his favorite cartoon character was. He said, "Yosemite Sam." I asked him to change the voice to Yosemite Sam. He did and began to laugh. I asked him to hear the original voice, make the changes, and then hear silence. He did this act five times. I encouraged him to practice this daily. When he returned the next week, he appeared very changed. His hair was clean and well groomed. He sat erect and looked me in the eye. Pat said that changing the voice of his ex-girlfriend had worked miracles. He felt like the old Pat, the one before that horrible relationship. Pat cured himself by taking the power away from the voice that was creating the depression. As with the visual, by changing the sub-modalities of the audio, the experience is changed.

The previous situations are examples of using NLP to resolve depression and anxiety. You can easily take your own situation and substitute it in each practice.

Observing Panic Attacks

Martha came to see me because of panic attacks. Currently in her senior year of college and looking toward Med School, she was scheduled to take the MCAT in a few weeks. Although she had no history of panic attacks, she was suddenly having them frequently. As Martha and I talked, she indicated that she was a very analytical person, approaching life from an intellectual perspective rather than an emotional perspective.

I suggested that she look at her panic attacks objectively. I asked her to take some deep breaths and relax. Then, I asked her to remember her last panic attack and begin to feel the sensations that she felt during this attack. I suggested that she just notice them as if she were observing something through a microscope. She was not to try to change the sensations but just to pay attention to them, study them, notice if any changes occurred, notice if they became more intense or less intense, notice if they moved to another location in her body, notice if the sensations changed to a different sensation, and notice what color and shape they were. She reported that they were purple in color and shaped like a jagged rectangle. They were located in her chest. The sensation was primarily one of pressure. It felt like her chest would explode. Over the period of the next fifteen minutes or so, the sensations shrunk to a smaller area of her chest, the pressure became significantly less, the edges of the rectangle smoothed out and the color changed to blue. She reported feeling far more relaxed than in the beginning. I suggested that she practice this several times a day and that if she had a panic attack, to use this exercise during the attack. When she returned the next week, she reported that she had had two panic attacks during the previous week but that she had done the exercise, and both times, they quickly abated. I saw her two more times, and she reported no more panic attacks.

When we fight our emotions, we will lose every time, but when we observe them and are mindful of them, they change. If Martha's feelings had not changed in a reasonable length of time, I would have asked her to make changes in the purple, jagged rectangle so that it would have appeared to look calm and confident instead of panicky.

The previous situation is an example of using a modified version of Mindfulness to resolve anxiety. It could also be effective for depression.

Tapping Her Anxiety Away

Robbie had grown up in a very dysfunctional family. As a result, during college, she developed anorexic tendencies and anxiety to the point of panic attacks. In our first session, I taught her to use the Emotional Freedom Technique. We walked through the process together. We tapped the sides of our hands eight to ten times, and as we tapped, she said, "Even though I have anxiety to the point of panic attacks, I completely and unconditionally accept myself." Then, we tapped above the inside corners of our eyebrows, beside our eyes, under our eyes, below our noses, on our chins, under our arms and on our chests. We tapped each spot eight to ten times. As we tapped these positions, Robbie would say a word related to her situation. She might say "anxiety" while tapping one point and "get well" while tapping another point. She was instructed to say whatever word came to her mind with each point. Then, we tapped between the knuckles of our little finger and our ring finger. As we tapped this point, Robbie looked down at the floor and gradually raised her eyes to the ceiling. Finally, she took several deep breaths. She had rated her anxiety an eight before we began the tapping process. As she rated it at the end, it had fallen to a four. We went through the process again and then added a new component. I asked her to close her eyes, open her eyes and look down to the right, then down to the left. Then, I asked her to rotate her eyes and then rotate them in the opposite direction. Finally, I asked her to hum "happy birthday," count to five, and then hum "happy birthday" again. Finally, we went through the tapping sequence again. When she rated her anxiety this time, it had fallen to a one. Her anxiety went from an eight to a one in less than an hour's time! Different tapping sequences have been developed for different problems, but I find that this general sequence seems to work effectively for most problems.

The previous example shows how Energy Psychology can be used to effectively eliminate anxiety. It could also be used for depression. For a visual instruction on how and where to tap, please watch this video on YouTube: https://www.youtube.com/watch?v=pAclBdj20ZU (*How to Tap with Jessica Ortner: Emotional Freedom Technique Informational Video*).

Rewiring the Brain for Happiness

Positive Psychology has shown us primary differences between happiness and depression. Happy people are grateful; depressed people are resentful. Happy people are optimistic; depressed people are pessimistic. Happy people feel in control of their lives; depressed people feel like victims. Knowing these differences can be used to effectively cure oneself of depression.

Kate had tragically lost her teenage son in a car wreck. She grieved as any mother would. However, five years later, she was still in the depths of despair and had been unable to resume a life remotely similar to the life she had lived previously. She was hardly able to get out of bed daily, much less do any daily chores or engage in social or religious activities. It took all the energy she could muster to come to see me. We talked about how happy she had been prior to the accident and how involved she had been in community and religious activities. She wanted this again. I explained the differences between happy people and depressed people and told her how I could see us working on this if she agreed, which she did.

First, I gave her a pad and pen and asked her to list ten people toward whom she felt some degree of gratitude. Then, I asked her to write one specific deed that each person had done for her beside each name. The deed must be specific. For example, she could not write that she was grateful to her mother because her mother always supported her. She must write a specific time when her mother supported her. After she completed this list, I asked her to choose one person on the list to whom she would write a one-page letter thanking the person for the deed. This was her assignment for next week. After writing the letter, she would get it laminated and bring it to our second session.

Second, I gave her a large rubber band and asked her to wear it. Every time she caught herself thinking a pessimistic thought, she would pop herself with the rubber band and change the thought to an optimistic one.

Third, I asked her to take the pad and pen and make a list of ten things she wanted to accomplish. After making the list, I asked her to rank them from easiest to accomplish to most diffi-cult to accomplish. We focused on the easiest one, discussed how long it would take to accomplish it, and wrote a completion time beside it. Her first item was to clean out her clothes closet, which was a disaster. She thought it would take a total of ten hours to get it in tip top shape. We decided that it would be realistic for her to spend two hours a day working on it.

When she left my office, she was obviously more energized than when she came. When she returned the following week, we read the letter together and talked about it. Her homework was to contact this person (her brother) and make an appointment without telling him why she wanted to see him. When she went to see him, she was to read the letter to him and then the two of them would talk about it and finally she would give it to him.

She reported that she had had fun with the rubber band. She had caught herself multiple times thinking pessimistically but had noticed that by week's end the number of times had declined considerably, and she felt more optimistic. She had accomplished her task of cleaning out her closet. It had been difficult to start, but by the last day, she had been excited to complete the task.

For the next week, we went to the second name on the list and to the second chore. After writing the third letter and going to visit the person and having achieved her third goal on her to-do list, she reported that she was feeling very energized and we both agreed that she didn't need to see me anymore. She would continue writing the letters and doing the chores. She had already removed the rubber band from her wrist because she had become an optimistic thinker.

It is much easier to achieve a positive goal than a negative goal. You cannot overcome depression by trying to get rid of it. Achieving the goal of being happy eliminates the depression. You cannot be happy and depressed at the same time. I have never used Positive Psychology with anxiety. I can imagine that it would be effective, but the other approaches work so well that I have never considered this approach in helping folks cure themselves of anxiety.

Summary

In closing this chapter, we want to give you in bullet format, the strategies that Buddy described:

- Changing the characteristics of a picture – You can mentally create a calm picture (for anxiety) or happy picture (for depression) and notice the sub-modality differences in the positive picture and the negative picture and then change the negative picture to be in the same location and have the same sub-modalities as the positive picture; or you can change the sub-modalities of the painful picture that give it power to take the power away. Remember to do this five times moving from the original picture to the new picture.

- Creating a well-defined audio visual of future success – Create a mental movie of being successful in those situations that create anxiety or depression and play it over and over. Be sure to make the movie as powerful as possible.

- Changing the sub-modalities of a voice – Change the location, volume, and tone of a negative voice by moving it out, turning down the volume, and changing it to a cartoon character.

- Observing the emotional pain instead of fighting it – Pay attention to where the pain is located in your body and the sensation of the pain (tingling, heat, cold, pressure, etc.). Don't try to change it; just notice it, and notice how it changes. It may change locations, intensity, or from one feeling to a different feeling. After ten minutes or so, if nothing has happened, you might notice the color of the sensation and slowly change it to a color that represents health to you. Many times, this produces instant results, but if not, continue until you do obtain results.

- Tapping exercise – Use the tapping algorithm described in the example earlier in this chapter. After using it several times, you can visualize doing the tapping (without actually doing it), and it will work just as effectively. See *How to Tap with Jessica Ortner: Emotional Freedom Technique Informational Video* on YouTube at the link listed previously in this chapter.

- The gratitude, optimism, and self-confidence exercises – Write the letters; pop yourself with a rubber band when you think a pessimistic thought, and change it to an optimistic thought; and make a list of things you want to accomplish, and then begin with the easiest one on the list.

Have fun experimenting with these techniques. The more you practice them, the more effective you will become in using them. May they bring you the same degree of satisfaction that they have brought so many others.

Chapter 2
Self-Compassion and Other Brain Changing Techniques

Habits are entrenched behaviors, but they are not impossible to change. Smoking is a prime example. While chemicals in the brain reward the smoking behavior, many smokers are able to break the addiction with nicotine replacement therapies like the patch or with drugs that block the reward center like Chantix. However, even after the physical addiction is broken, new habits have to be learned. Smokers often say they have to do something with their hands or learn to take a walk right after a meal when they used to smoke. At first, these new habits require a lot of work, but eventually, the brain creates a new normal that doesn't involve smoking. Other well-known and common examples include learning to walk with a prosthetic or relearning to talk after a stroke. While we have plenty of examples of how our bodies can physically rewire the brain, the same process can happen in the brain with our thoughts.

Often thoughts that lead to depression, anxiety, and compulsion or dependence are well-worn pathways. Life coach Lorrainne Faendrich, who specializes in mind-body techniques, calls these "lizard thoughts." They are our fearful, survival mode thoughts that drive many of our emotions and actions. We believe these thoughts are our only option, but it turns out they are only a small portion of the possible thoughts we could have about the same experience.

Often, the old neuropathways were helpful to us at one time. For example, a child who is abused may have to dissociate from trauma in order to survive the ordeal at the time. However, once the child is grown and safely away from the situation, the pathway of dissociation is no longer useful. In fact, it causes more of its own trauma. Another example is teaching children that hard work is a virtue. It is a virtue when you are trying to get through school and begin a job, but that same virtue can become a vice or an impediment to a joyful life for workaholics. Fear of failure can be a motivating factor, but it can also leave us in constant motion and search for success after success. Drinking to relax is initially effective, but as it becomes the only way a person can calm down, it becomes harmful. Teaching the brain another way to face the same situation provides long-lasting and powerful implications.

We discussed mindfulness in the previous chapter as one way to retrain the brain, but there are other specific practices people often find useful. Rewiring how we view events, react to emotional situations, or interact with our families and friends are powerful tools. Neuroplasticity is a big buzzword, but it isn't just trendy. We used to think we were subject to our genes, our personalities, or our neuroses, but science is beginning to tell us that we actually have the power to change the way our brains work!

In this chapter, we will share some of the most effective tools from our practices for rewiring the brain.

Self-Compassion

As mentioned in the preface, Lynn is good at getting participants to treat themselves with the same compassion they would bestow on someone they care about. When we picture ourselves as someone we really care about, a child, a good friend, or a family member, we are oftentimes more understanding than we are with our own person.

The shift in perspective is powerful. We would never berate our child or a friend the way we do ourselves for the very same thoughts or actions. We reach out to comfort others in their times of distress, even when they have screwed up royally. Following this activity, Lynn asked participants to write a letter to themselves using the same language they wrote down toward another person. This is the practice of self-compassion. Here is an example of one letter from this workshop:

Dear Sophia,

You have had a tough few years. A divorce and single parenting are big life events. I want you to know that I know you try hard. I want you to know that, even if you try your hardest, you are going to screw up sometimes. This isn't a free pass for all your mistakes, but through your mistakes, if you are honest about them, you learn. Every day you learn to be a better mom.

You really should look at taking some time for yourself to learn how to cope with stressful situations more appropriately. Given your childhood, it is not surprising that you don't have many coping skills. But, don't pass that lack of learning down another generation. You can do it. Start exercising, like you want to. Start eating better. Ask for help with the kids. Don't feel guilty taking time to take care of yourself. It will make you a less-angry mom.

I want you to know I love you and that you are special. Many women would have given up where you dug deep. You are incredibly tough and I'm proud of you.

Love,
Sophia

Self-Compassion currently receives a lot of attention. It is often dismissed as an excuse for narcissism in an iProduct, selfie-obsessed culture, but techniques of self-compassion are gaining traction across age groups because of the positive effects they create. Dr. Kristin Neff is the budding guru on self-compassion as an effective practice. In an article entitled "Why Self-Compassion Trumps Self-Esteem," she writes that while criticizing ourselves and beating ourselves up is socially sanctioned, it isn't all that helpful in creating change. What does create change is self-compassion. She says,

> Over the past decade, research that my colleagues and I have conducted shows that self-compassion is a powerful way to achieve emotional well-being and contentment in our lives, helping us avoid destructive patterns of fear, negativity, and isolation. More so than self-esteem, the nurturing quality of self-compassion allows us to flourish, to appreciate the beauty and richness of life, even in hard times. When we soothe our agitated minds with self-compassion, we're better able to notice what's right as well as what's wrong, so that we can orient ourselves toward that which gives us joy.

If we accept that learning to cultivate a little self-compassion might be a good thing despite the fact that most of us have been taught that it is a selfish endeavor, how do we do it? What will it do for us if we use these techniques? Dr. Neff provides a list of exercises on her website of techniques you can use at home today to increase your ability for self-compassion. These include writing, self-talk, and listening exercises designed to turn your inner voice from critic to advocate. Almost every exercise uses the three-component model Neff has identified through research to increase self-compassion. These include becoming aware of critical emotions and thoughts (mindfulness), identifying with common humanity, and reacting with acceptance and encouragement. For example, her exercise "Identifying What We Really Want" asks you to think about ways you use critical thought to motivate you to get things done. We often tell ourselves that we are lazy or fundamentally flawed when we think about food. We think that berating ourselves will make us stick to our diets. In fact, the opposite is often true. Neff encourages people to find a kinder, more caring way to motivate the same action or change and notice the pain that their self-judgment causes.

One of our favorite stories on the power of radical self-compassion comes from a woman named Molly. Molly struggled with her weight her whole life. She writes, "I haven't always been so friendly with my body. As a matter of fact, I can hardly remember a time when I wasn't in a battle with it. At a very young age I learned that my body wasn't acceptable. I dieted, over-exercised, starved and binged on unhealthy food. I tried to change my body and found that it rebelled riotously. It grew bigger, got sick and I grew angrier." One day, Molly gave up her battle and took a new tactic. She decided to try something she had never thought possible before. "Then a few years ago I got tired of not liking myself, of being angry with my body for not being what other people told me it should be. I was exhausted and sad. I began to wonder what would happen if I just accepted that this was my body and it deserved love and kindness. It deserved to be well fed and exercised and to feel pleasure. I wondered what would happen if instead of hating my body I loved it and was thankful for it. And so began my grand experiment."

Molly's experiment exceeded beyond her wildest hopes. Is she thin now? No. But she is confident, healthy, and comfortable in her own skin for the first time in her life. She says,

> Instead of dismissing what our body is telling us we need to listen. When we need rest, we need to rest and when we need exercise, exercise. Taking the time to eat good food and not easy food

is important. Treating ourselves to a slice of cake or latte with real milk can be rejuvenating. We do deserve pleasure. Our bodies crave it. Dance, hold your head up and walk with confidence and look people in the eye. And allow yourself to be seen, admired and touched. It doesn't happen overnight but with practice and patience and openness to your own value it happens.

Neff concludes, "Remember that if you really want to motivate yourself, love is more powerful than fear." Self-compassion techniques succeed in teaching us how to help ourselves just as effectively as we are able to help those we care about. Training your brain to choose a compassionate response doesn't happen overnight, but it is possible with practice. Molly's story is a powerful one about how the simple act of training our brains to become advocates, rather than critics, changes everything.

Changing Your Thoughts

Because we have learned that rewiring the brain is possible, we need to look for exercises that help us make these changes. Buddy Wagner described several in the last chapter. We would like to add several more techniques to your toolkit.

Listening to Pain

Another way to rewire the brain is to listen to our emotions. As discussed earlier in this book, we spend an inordinate amount of time trying to numb, fight, distract, or avoid our emotions. We just want our negative emotions to go away and leave us alone. Ironically, one of the best ways to get them to leave may be to listen to them. Therapist Lorraine Faehndrich once told Alison in a webinar interview, "Our emotions are always trying to tell us something important. When we listen to them and they know we get the message, then they will leave."

Mindfulness researchers agree. They encourage us to
our emotions and physical pains, not run away from them
practice, we sink into our bodies, identify the emotion or physical
pain, and ask it what it is trying to tell us. Then, no matter how
odd our answers seem, we write them down.

One of the most well-researched success stories of listening to
pain come from dealing with back problems. John Sarno's work
on why back pain is a distracting play by the mind on the body is
impressive. The pain distracts us from the emotions that need to
be heard. Once these emotions are identified, the back pain often
disappears. In his most recent work, Sarno takes the hyphen out
of mindbody and includes anxiety and depression in his grouping
of disorders that can be alleviated by refusing to let the subconscious mind distract us from the real issues. He says we are simply one, not the mind and the body but the mindbody.

An example of how listening to emotional pain relieves emotional distress comes from a woman we interviewed about chronic fatigue. Amy said, "I could not get over my exhaustion or fog-
giness. I tried to eat better, rest more, sleep longer, but nothing
worked. When I tried the exercise of listening to my emotion, I
didn't really expect relief. I settled into the fog around my brain,
gently asked it what it wanted, and the most surprising thing
came up. I lost a brother as a child and had never really dealt
with it. When I started moving through the emotions of that
event, my energy returned."

What does your pain, fatigue, mood, or mental state really
want to tell you? Getting still and listening is the first step in
finding out. Moving that information out of your head and onto
paper is an extremely effective therapeutic process. Sarno says,
"do-gooders, high achievers, and people who need to be liked
are especially susceptible to rage in their subconscious" because
the ego doesn't want these things. The ego is self-centered, a bit
lazy, and concerned with feeling good and rage is the result. Once
we quit letting our bodies distract us with physical problems or

mental health problems, we become well. Sarno believes you can achieve this by writing down the things that upset or anger you daily. Just let it fly on paper and tell yourself, "I know these things are the reason for my problem, not (fill in the blank: depression, neck pain, autoimmune conditions.)" You may be surprised at what you uncover.

Setting an Anchor

Setting an anchor was another powerful process Buddy introduced in a session on The Mind-Body Connection. Setting an anchor allows you to switch on your high-performance or positive emotional state at will. According to research that Buddy shared with us by O'Connor and Seymore, setting an anchor is a simple process. Get comfortable. Think of a situation in which you would like to be different, feel different, and respond differently—for example, when your children misbehave. Next, choose a particular emotional state that you would most like to have available to you in that situation. It can be any resourceful state—confidence, humor, courage, persistence, creativity—whatever comes to mind as being most appropriate. If it is difficult to remember a time when you experienced a positive state, then picture yourself on a movie screen operating in that imagined state. Now choose your anchor.

The anchor can be kinesthetic, like tapping your fingers together or making a fist. Buddy reminded participants that athletes often do this by touching the bottom of their shoes or a sidewall to bring back a feeling of confidence after a bad play. It can be auditory, like a word or a phrase you say to yourself. Some people call this a mantra or an intention. The word doesn't matter as long as it is attached to the desired feeling. The anchor can also be visual. It can be a symbol that you see in your mind or carry in your wallet. Bestselling author and philanthropist Glennon Doyle Melton has her anchor tattooed on her hand. It says, "Be Still."

Use your anchor whenever you get into a situation where you need it. The anchor can become almost automatic and is a fast way to get your body and mind to respond the way you want it to.

Rewiring the Brain Through Intentions and Visualization

Remember the book, *The Power of Positive Thinking*, by Norman Vincent Peale? What a great strategy for improving your life. Who could argue with the fact that people who "think positive thoughts" are happier? The problem for people with depression, anxiety, and addiction issues is that they don't often know how to think positive thoughts. Alison remembers in the depths of her depression before going on medication, her dad had sent her a book called *Feeling Good*! By David Burns. Alison had imagined the exclamation point in the title with Mr. Burns' smiling face mocking her from the cover, and she thought, "Well, wouldn't that be nice!" But, feeling good for her was the problem. Alison had no more hope of forcing herself to feel good or think positive thoughts than she could have hoped to dunk a basketball.

Turns out, she might have been wrong. Setting intentions is a powerful way to rewire the brain to think the thoughts that will create positive emotions. But, the way you set intentions is important. You can't just say, "I am happy," and expect a magical change to occur. What is an intention anyway? Is it just a trendy word for a goal?

If you listen closely, you will hear a lot about intentions from successful people who seem to use them intuitively to shape their lives. Oprah uses the word to describe how she bloomed in her career. Jim Carey recently said he used intentions to create his dream life. Are intentions just fanciful wishes, or an egomaniac's fixation on a certain outcome? You won't find research on the power of setting intentions in mainstream journals, but when you talk to successful people, they all seem to consciously lay out what it is they want to bring into their lives. For our purposes, we will say setting intentions are like drawing a roadmap of where you want to go. Isn't it possible or even likely that following a different roadmap than your old depressed, anxious, or addicted map might lead you somewhere better? Isn't it possible or even probable that if you continued to use that new map, your brain might discover and adopt new and healthier tools?

It takes practice to set intentions effectively. They are more than just goals or behaviors you will perform to meet those goals. New-age guru Dr. Deepak Chopra says, "Intentions are the start of every dream." However, setting intentions isn't just for new-age, spiritual seekers. Nicky Roche, who has held senior management positions in three multinational companies hosted a podcast called "Setting Your Business Intentions for 2016." She says, "Intentions are less tangible than business goals, but incredibly important. They deal with the *perspective* you view yourself, and your business and the opportunity from, in this next year. Intentions bring about transformations in the way that you think.... and this will transform your business." This practice can easily be applied to your personal life.

In her article in the *Huffington Post*, Stephenie Zamora says, "Talking is great. Action is awesome. Intention is everything." People who use intentions as a way to manifest the things they want in their lives do it in a specific manner. The Chopra Center encourages four steps for setting intentions. Becoming fully aware of the present moment, or meditating, is the first step to setting intention because it allows you to remove your ego and listen to what your heart really wants. Once you are in this state, release your intention and desires without monitoring them. Next, remain in a state of restful awareness after you set the intention. This means refusing to be influenced by doubts and criticism. Finally, detach from the outcome and let the universe handle the details.

There are literally hundreds of guided mediations on setting intentions available at no cost online. I like bestselling author Tara Brach, who offers a guided audio clip on setting intentions on her website. Former Wall Street shark turned dean of the Chopra Center, Davidji, also has many great tools for setting intentions on his website at www.davidji.com. In one exercise, he says, "Get clear on what you want and write it down. Share with someone you trust—this will hold you accountable. Do something today that demonstrates your commitment. And, acknowledge that you did what you said you were going to do."

We do have some science on the power of intention from the field of sports. Professional athletes are trained in visualizations and positive self-talk to improve their game. Golf writer David MacKenzie says, "The world's best athletes use the practice of visualizing a great performance before the action for a very good reason—it works!" It appears that the brain does not know the difference between visualizing an action and actually performing it. In other words, visualizing your free throw effectively lights up the same parts of the brain as actually standing on the line and shooting.

Emily Cook of the U.S. Olympic Ski Team says, "When I'm doing visualization before an event I make sure to include all of my senses." The kinesthetic component of visualization is important for athletes. They have to feel the muscles being used, hear the buzzing of the crowd, and see the entire process complete perfectly. In business, professionals use visualizations prior to presentations.

Creating our own visualizations is easy with vision boards. In this exercise, you cut out pictures of the things you want to manifest in your life within a set time period. These images are specific. Then, you hang the board somewhere where you can see it daily. The woman who introduced us to vision boards, Dottie Porter, told us, "I've done one board every New Year's for thirty years. It is amazing to look at the old board at the end of each year and see all the things I made happen in my life."

Intentions and visualization create intense focus which ultimately helps rewire the brain so that it is able to imagine and then take the steps necessary to make those goals a reality in our lives. Comedian Steve Harvey spoke about the power of intentions to override reality in an address to the business college at Mississippi State University. He grew up poor and with a significant speech impediment. His teacher ridiculed him in front of the class when he said he wanted to grow up and be on television. He wasn't deterred. He said, "I can't explain it any other way than that I saw myself as a T.V. celebrity and I believed in that vision." He concluded by saying, "And, I make sure to send that teacher a new flat screen every year so she is sure not to miss me!"

What could setting intentions for the changes we want to see in our lives do for people with depression or anxiety? What physical changes in our brains could occur over time if we could sincerely imagine a different way of being? What steps would we be able to take toward manifesting this new reality in our lives? If we look at the winners, the people who seem truly happy with their lives, who are able to make a difference, it is clear that intentions and visualizations are worth looking into and incorporating into our rituals.

Summary

Using the techniques from this chapter can help us retrain our minds with new and healthy patterns. Depression and anxiety are the results of thought patterns that lead to negative emotions. Even though addiction is classified as a disease and undoubtedly contains a physical component, a lifetime of behaviors and thoughts fuel its progress. When we learn to separate from our thoughts, identify the ones that are harmful, and replace them with healthy ones, we can really make progress toward shaping our brains in positive ways.

Whether we can change our brains permanently is not yet clear, but the fact that we can alter our paths at all is revolutionary! The most exciting part about the techniques we have shared in this chapter is that they are either free or inexpensive and that the only negative side effect is that they might not work for you. Whether they work or not seems to come down to two factors: effort and belief. The power of expectation greatly impacts the results of using these techniques. Skeptics don't report much progress with these tools, likely because they do not use them or do not stick with them, but for those who open their minds up to the possibilities, the rewards are often amazing. Why not take a chance if the worst you could be is wrong? Why not choose the technique that appeals to you the most and commit to two weeks of working through the process? When your situation brings you to the point of having nothing left to lose, it is a gift. That is usually the point when we open our heart and minds and say, "Okay, it's worth a try."

We want to give you a summary of the techniques presented in this chapter for easy reference:

- Self-Compassion – write a letter to yourself, picture yourself as a child, find more on Dr. Sarah Neff's website: http://self-compassion.org/category/exercises
- Listening to Pain – using guided meditations, identifying what the body tells us, moving that information out of the body through writing
- Setting an Anchor – choose a kinesthetic, visual, or audio anchor that can quickly place you in the state of emotion you want
- Visualization and Affirmations – creating vision boards, making simple affirmative statements, imagining what could be and then taking the steps to make it happen

If we think we are stuck with our mental illnesses because of our genes, learning that we can actually change our brains is incredibly good news. Science is on our side, and the discoveries of neuroplasticity bring a whole new field of possibilities to mental health and addiction. According to Seigel in *The Mindful Therapist* (2010), "Findings from science now confirm the notion that the mind can activate the brain's circuitry in ways that change the brain's structural connections. In other words, you can use the subjective inner aspect of reality to alter the objective physical structure of the brain. We can use the mind to transform our brains and our lives." When we can change our brains, the possibilities for creating happy, productive lives, in spite of mental health and mood disorder challenges, expands tremendously.

Chapter 3
A Spiritual Approach

We are spiritual beings. This statement will have different meanings for each person who reads it. Some may put a religious spin on it. Some may put a secular spin on it. Some may equate it with the unconscious mind. Some may see it being totally in the affective realm—the area of human experience dealing with feelings, attitudes, and emotions. Some may shy away from the word "spiritual" altogether, but we suspect they still think and talk about it, using a different vocabulary. We will equate it primarily with the unconscious mind but also, at times, put a religious spin on it.

Spiritual development makes us stop and examine the affective or subconscious realms of our lives, and because our actions are so often driven by our beliefs, even if they are subconscious, spiritual growth is worth looking at in overcoming anxiety and depression. It is a discipline of self-care that often enables people to find meaning and feel connected to something larger than themselves.

Buddy was raised in a religious home. His family was in the local Baptist Church every time the doors were opened. Throughout most of his boyhood and teen years, he planned to be a Baptist minister. He learned to think, believe, and speak the religious language of his particular denomination, and he still uses some of this vocabulary and holds on to some of those early teachings. When he was trained in hypnosis and Neuro Linguistic Programming, he learned about the power of the unconscious mind and continues to discover how rich and powerful it is. This chapter will give you his thoughts and experiences on how spirituality can help heal anxiety and depression.

Prayer

I must confess that even though I have prayed most of my life, I did not believe that it made much difference in helping people heal themselves of pain until I read *Prayer Is Good Medicine* by Larry Dossey, who is a medical doctor. Like me, Dossey was skeptical of prayer making any difference in folks getting well. However, his patients kept telling him stories of prayer healing people, so he decided to look at the research to see if there was any proof. He did not expect to find much and expected that what he did find would not be good research. To his surprise, there was far more than he expected and much of it had been done by universities and other reputable bodies. The research indicated several truths, two of which I shall mention. First, prayer is effective in creating healing. Dossey points out that everyone who prays is not healed, just as no medical practice is one-hundred-percent effective; but healing does occur a significant amount of the time. Second, prayer is effective regardless of the religious faith, or lack thereof, of the one doing the praying.

After reading Dossey's book and reflecting on my own spiritual experiences, I became convinced that prayer could make a difference in healing from anxiety or depression. Some might be offended by my not giving God, Jahweh, Allah, etc. the credit for the healing. I believe that all healing comes from a higher power, but I believe that we have all been created by this higher power with the innate ability to heal ourselves of many of the discomforts we experience. Therefore, I recommend that as part of your healing process, you include prayer in whatever form is meaningful for you.

Mindful Meditation

Taking time each day to quiet your mind for several minutes by focusing your attention inward can make a huge difference in your depression or anxiety. I believe this is a spiritual experience because it seems to go deeper than our thoughts and feelings. We get in touch with a deeper part of ourselves. You can use the exercise given in the Mindfulness section of the chapter on Neuro Linguistic Programming or spend time merely focusing on your breathing. You may only be able to sit quietly for two or three minutes initially but keep practicing every day and you will eventually lengthen your time. I would encourage you to work up to twenty minutes a day. Don't get upset when your mind wanders, gently bring it back to your present focus.

Learning to separate yourself from your thoughts is a vital step in overcoming anxiety and depression. You have thoughts constantly, and when you are anxious or depressed, those thoughts cycle over and over saying the same things. Mindful Meditation helps you recognize those incessant thoughts, separate from them so that they lose their emotional charge, and sink below or rise above them to a place of serenity.

Positive Visualization

In Robert Dilts' book *Belief: Pathway to Health and Well-Being*, he tells the story of his mother. She had cancer and had been through treatment. The doctors told her that they had done all they could do and that she had a limited time to live. Among other actions that she took, she began to focus her attention inward to her cancer every day. She pictured the cancer as grass and her immune system as sheep eating the grass. When she went back to her doctor for a checkup he could not find any traces of the cancer. She lived another thirteen-and-a-half years. Obviously, every story does not end like this, but who's to say that your story with depression or anxiety cannot be similar to hers.

Allow me to share a personal story with you. I have a mole on the left side of my face and another one on the right side of my neck. They protruded out enough that I would cut them when I shaved if I were not careful. One day, I cut one of them, and it occurred to me that maybe I could resolve this problem mentally. Each morning, before I shaved I would spend several minutes focusing my attention on the moles and visualizing them going away. I did this for several weeks. Several months later, it occurred to me that I had not cut one of the moles in several weeks. I looked more closely and realized that they had not gone away but they had shrunk to the point that they are no longer a problem.

I don't know how to explain this scientifically, but in my work over the years, I have become more and more convinced that the body has an amazing ability to heal itself based on the beliefs one holds.

Using Sacred Writings

Sacred writings can be used as metaphors or used literally to help one overcome anxiety or depression. I will focus on Bible passages in this section because these are the sacred writings with which I am familiar, but all sacred writings can be helpful. This would include the sacred writings of Islam, Buddhism, and all other religious faiths. I would recommend that you select two or three passages that are most meaningful and comforting to you and spend a few minutes every day reading them and meditating on them.

Anxiety is basically caused by living in the future. This paraphrased story from Exodus could help you recognize the need to let go of the future and focus on the present: While the Israelites were traveling toward the promised land, they became hungry, and they complained to Moses that not only did they not have food stored up for tomorrow, but they had nothing to eat today. Moses asked God to provide food for them. Each morning the ground was covered with manna from heaven. They were only to take enough for that day. If they gathered more than a day's need, it would not be edible the next day. Even though they always had enough, many wanted more than a day's need. They weren't satisfied with having enough now. They were concerned about the future and what would happen tomorrow. Those who worried about tomorrow lived in misery, while those who focused on the present were content and happy.

This Bible passage is a good reminder that worry and anxiety make no difference. It is much more profitable to focus on what is positive.

> *(Matthew 6:25-34)* Look at the birds of the air; they do not sow and reap and store in barns, but they have plenty to eat. Can you increase your height by worrying about it? Look at the lilies in the field. They do not work but they are clothed beautifully. Set your mind on what is good and wholesome and you will experience the peace of heaven.

When you feel anxious or fearful, it can feel as if you are at sea and a storm is raging. You may doubt that you can survive. But, by taking one minute at a time and being sure to maintain your strength, the storm eventually abates and land appears. Find a sacred text that helps you put anxiety into perspective. Write it down. Carry it with you, pin it to your mirror, or memorize it. Spend some time with the passage each day.

The darkness of depression can last for weeks or months, but it will not last forever. Change will occur. The Bible is filled with stories of people who were in despair just before things changed drastically. For Christians, the resurrection story is the paramount example of new life after the darkest hour.

Another example is in the book of Kings. Elijah became depressed because he thought he was about to die at the hands of Queen Jezebel. He prayed to die. He felt worthless. All he wanted to do was sleep. His mind was filled with negative thoughts convincing him that he was all alone and that no one cared about him. He endured many mental storms, and it seemed as if the ground were moving out from under his feet. He felt shaky with no firm foundation. His head and his heart were burning as if they were on fire. Somehow, he began to quiet his mind, and as it became calmer, he realized that he had much to live for. Friends came to mind, and he began to see purpose in his life again. His energy was renewed, and he began to live.

Sacred passages also show us how universal depression and suffering are. In Psalm 31, the Psalmist asked for grace because he was in distress. He was in so much grief that it affected his eyesight. His energy was zapped by sorrow. He stumbled under a heavy load of misery. His sadness had made him physically ill. He believed that people scorned him and that he was such a burden to his friends that they dreaded to see him coming. He felt lost. Then, a miracle occurred, and he found himself. In the end, he was able to say to others to be strong and to have courage. There is always hope, no matter how hopeless life seems.

A story in Joel paints a vivid picture of depression and gives hope by demonstrating that life is hard, beautiful, and cyclical. I paraphrase it like this: All joy and gladness are gone. The soil is parched, the dykes are dry, the granaries are deserted, the barns are ruinous, and rains have failed. The cattle are exhausted, and the oxen are distressed because they have no pasture. The flocks of sheep waste away. The earth shakes, the heavens shudder, and the sun and moon are darkened. The stars no longer shine. Yet, life is gracious and compassionate. It is always ready to turn things around and heap blessings on you. The rains can come again, and the crops can be renewed. The animals can have plenty to eat, and the sun, moon and stars can shine again. Joy and gladness can return.

There is no magic in contemplating these passages or stories. Or is there? I wonder what would happen if you took several minutes a day to pay attention to the hope that these writings give. Why not try it and see?

Bob suffered from anxiety. He had been hospitalized a couple of times and was on anti-anxiety medication when he came to see me. He and I did several things together to help his anxiety, one of which was to focus our attention on several verses from the book of Matthew ending, "Therefore do not worry about tomorrow, for tomorrow will worry about itself. Each day has enough trouble of its own." He copied this passage onto a three by five card and kept it in his wallet. Every morning, he would take it out and spend several minutes focusing on it. Anytime he began to feel anxious, he would take it out and focus his attention on it. Doing this exercise, along with the other exercises he learned, helped him conquer his anxiety. He eventually was able to stop taking medication and reports that he remains calm and peaceful most of the time. He continues to carry the card in his wallet and uses it when he needs it. He claims that it is a big help.

Summary

Often, our beliefs shape what we see and how we behave. Developing a spiritual practice that emphasizes hope can be an important piece of the wellness puzzle. In closing this chapter, we want to give you in bullet format the exercises Buddy explained:

- Use sacred writings by focusing your attention on those that give you hope
- Use prayer (whatever this means to you) as part of your healing process
- Practice Mindful Meditation to separate from your thoughts, quiet your mind, and delve deeper
- Visualize yourself bringing about healing

You have far more internal abilities than you can imagine. You have been wonderfully created! Trust your spiritual self to bring about healing through the above exercises. You can heal yourself!

Chapter 4
Stress and its Antidotes

Throughout history, stress has served an important, specific function: it tries to protect us from perceived threats. For most of human history, stress kept us alive and alert, watching for dangers from nature or other humans. This incredible survival mechanism causes our heart rates to increase, our senses to become ultra-alert, our hearts to pump more oxygen into our muscles, and our livers to release extra energy in the form of sugar. You are ready to fight for your life, play dead, or run for it.

Today, stress is less useful when we see imaginary threats behind every building, or when your boss or spouse causes your fight or flight response to kick in. Our bodies and minds cannot distinguish between our spouse yelling at us and a tiger attacking. And, what one person can shrug off, another may perceive as threatening (even though they may not identify it this way logically). Getting a bad grade, receiving criticism, thinking there is not enough time to get everything done, handling financial problems, and dealing with illnesses all cause stress to varying degrees.

While it may be easier to identify the effects of stress on people in poverty or people dealing with traumatic situations, it is not always easy to reconcile our own first world, insured, not-currently-under-threat-of-war reactions to the world. In fact, many of us don't even see that we are experiencing stress because we think the conditions in our lives are normal. It takes learning to get in touch with your body to recognize that stress rules much of our day. Once we wake up to the possibility, it becomes easier to notice the scrunched shoulders, the increased heart rate, the clenched stomach in response to things like someone calling in the middle of a busy moment. Seemingly silly incidents, like finding an error in an email, can send a tingle to a sore spot in our backs. Bigger things, like a fight with our kids, can send waves of heat streaming from our guts.

Jon Kabat-Zinn calls this "Full Catastrophe Living," in his landmark book covering his research at the University of Massachusetts Medical Center. Full catastrophe living is exactly how many of us live every single day. We develop very effective coping mechanisms to deal with it temporarily. Some of us choose numbing behaviors. Others escape, attack, or curl up and play dead. People cope in different ways. Some exercise, others eat, or scroll, or shop, or work too much. Alcohol and pills serve as antidotes to a day filled with stress. Some people just roll over and play dead, develop chronic illnesses, or take to the bed to deal with stress.

It doesn't even matter if the event is stressful from an objective standpoint. What matters is whether or not you perceive the event as stressful. Once your brain perceives a threat, it immediately sends a signal to your adrenal glands telling them to release adrenaline. Your brain also sends signals to the pituitary gland that tell the body to release cortisol. Cortisol keeps your sugar and blood pressure up, ready to fight or flee. Your muscles tense, full of oxygen, and your body directs all resources away from things like fertility and digestion and move toward survival. Oftentimes, we don't know why we are reacting so strongly to seemingly inconsequential events, but can you imagine what that constant release of cortisol and adrenaline do to the body year after year?

What chronic stress does to the body over time is well documented. Weight gain, cardiovascular disease, chronic fatigue, chronic pain, and mood disorders all result from our bodies being exhausted from dealing ineffectively with stress. Many of our nervous systems, not to mention our immune systems, are just plain shot.

In this chapter, the authors want to give you tools that help you manage stress in healthy ways. These techniques help you identify your stressors and put them in context. Don't judge yourself if you are a person who reacts strongly to seemingly insignificant stressors. Your body cannot distinguish between what counselors call, "little t's and Big T's"—little traumas and big traumas. All of us need to come to a new understanding about how to face stress and know that we do not have to go numb, escape, fight, or play dead in order to live with it.

Identify Your Stressors

As we have mentioned before, writing or journaling is an excellent way to concretely separate yourself from your thoughts. Journaling takes your thoughts out of your head and places them outside your body where you may be able to look at them more objectively. In a notebook or a journal, take a page, sink into a quiet spot for a few minutes, and ask yourself, "What are my stressors?"

List the big ones, but also list any small factors that come up. Don't judge them. They may seem silly, and maybe they are, but your body doesn't know that. Now, ask yourself, "Where do I hold stress in my body?"

Many people hold stress in their shoulders, backs, or stomachs. Some hold it in their jaw or around their eyes. Finding out where you hold stress in your body helps us connect to the physical impact stress has on you. It makes stress easier to identify when it arises.

On the next page, list out how you deal with stress. Do you exercise, scroll through social media, take time to yourself, travel, work too much, watch television, shop, yell, drink, or take pills? Some of these coping mechanisms will be healthy, others will not be. Place a star by the coping mechanisms that are healthy. Then, read through the rest of the chapter and decide what other stress busting behaviors you would like to adopt. Come back to your journal and write those down.

Exercise

Your body has to have a method for discharging stress that builds up in the body. We have learned that animals do this by shaking. When they are attacked in the wild and escape, they tremor the muscles that were used in the fight or flight response. They shake visibly. Humans have lost our ability to "shake off stress," but we have another effective mechanism. Physical activity decreases stress and improves mood, causes the body to release soothing chemicals into the bloodstream, and takes your mind off the object of worry or depression.

Getting moving is hard, but once you move, you will feel better. It may help to lower your expectations about exercise. It doesn't have to look like a marathon race or an aerobics class at the gym (unless those things really appeal to you). Choose an activity you love, or one that you have to do anyway in your daily routine. For example, taking the stairs at work or in your apartment, walking the dog, or parking far away from stores is a simple way to build movement into your routine. Dancing around the house or even house cleaning to music can get your heart-rate up. Try tai-chi, swimming, or yoga, which are gentler forms of exercise.

Whatever form you choose, make sure you like it, or you can automate it so that you stick with the routine. You need thirty minutes a day, three times a week, to reduce anxiety or depression and five or more times a week for best results, but if you aren't doing anything, start with smaller goals and work up.

Mindfulness

What is mindfulness? It's simply a form of meditation that focuses the mind on the present moment. Why is this seemingly simple practice receiving so much attention? According to a paper by the American Psychological Association summarizing the research on mindfulness, the practice offers extraordinary results in several areas including: reduced worry, reduced stress, improved working memory and focus, decreased emotional reactivity, increased cognitive flexibility, and boosted immune system.

If mindfulness is so incredible, why isn't everyone doing it? The truth is, almost every major medical research institute is using mindfulness training now for everything from chronic pain management to lowering the risk for heart attacks. Mindfulness is starting to reach the rest of us, but we are resistant for several reasons. First, it's hard! The idea of quieting our chattering minds seems so impossible to us that we don't even attempt it. Second, we aren't convinced that it will work. The results are subtle, and sometimes hard to measure, and we don't want to waste our time. Third, there is often a cultural wariness around mindfulness and meditation in Western culture. We have encountered reluctance from people who believe meditation is counter to their religions. "I'm Christian. We don't do mindfulness." This argument is unfounded when you dig into the history of Christianity. Jesus meditated throughout the gospels, and there is a strong tradition of Centering Prayer that is a form of mindfulness used by Christians all over the world. And finally, we are busy. Taking even fifteen minutes out of our day to practice mindfulness proves difficult to nearly impossible for those of us who spend our days running from one activity to the next.

Whatever your reason, we are asking you to suspend judgement and try it for thirty days. What do you have to lose? If you don't have time during the day, set the alarm for fifteen minutes earlier and practice before your feet hit the floor. You can practice as you are falling asleep at night or during a lunch break. Everyone has fifteen minutes. Just make it part of your routine.

But how do you do mindfulness? Good question. There are a lot of varieties of mindfulness and meditation out there. We suggest you start with guided meditation. There are hundreds of free guided meditations videos on YouTube. A client, Mandy, used to listen to a free guided meditation for about a minute, and if it didn't drive her too crazy, she subscribed to that channel so she could find it again. If the person's voice or what they were saying grated on her, she sat up and moved on to the next video. Some of our favorites are The Honest Guys, The Chopra Center, and Tara Brach. There are also some great phone apps like Head Space and Five Minute Meditation. You can also find a yoga class. Most yoga classes end with a ten-minute meditation. In addition, there are most likely several churches in your area that host centering prayer groups.

When it comes to lowering your reactivity or your fight or flight response, the trick to meditation and mindfulness is consistency. Pick a time and make it part of your daily routine. Once you find a form you like, stick to it for thirty days. See if you can't begin to sink into your body when you feel attacked and notice what your body is doing. Then, as the "father of mindfulness," Thich Nhat Hanh, says to send that reaction a smile. Don't judge it, just smile and say, "I feel stress manifesting in my body." Record your stress levels in your journal, and see if you don't begin to notice a difference in your mood overall.

Food

Certain foods increase stress in the body, while others lower the stress hormone. Contrary to what we believe, chocolate does not make us feel better (for more than five minutes.) Some of the foods we turn to for comfort are the worst culprits when it comes to increasing stress levels. Energy drinks, coffee, and alcohol are all bad choices when it comes to lowering the stress hormone in our bodies. Unhealthy fats, sugar, and salt all increase cortisol levels, which kicks in our fight or flight response. Elevated cortisol over the long term consistently produces glucose, leading to increased blood sugar levels, weight gain, and an exhausted adrenal system.

Learning to develop healthy coping mechanisms for stress ultimately decreases the number of unhealthy foods we rely on. Some healthy food habits that lower stress include: drinking a cup of caffeine-free herbal tea, eating dark chocolate with more than eighty percent cocoa, taking omega-3 supplements or eating fatty fish. Some carbohydrates are healthy and help lower cortisol. Look into ancient grains such as spelt, amaranth, or polenta, and find an oatmeal that soothes you and your stress level. Increasing your leafy greens means you are getting more magnesium, which is a muscle and nerve relaxer.

Most of us rush through meals or eat on the run. Make eating into a ritual. Take your time. Use the pretty dishes. Sit down and chew slowly. Create several healthy food rituals, like cooking with your kids or your spouse. The way we eat, in addition to the foods we choose, can influence our levels of stress.

Sleep

Sleep is so important for wellbeing. Many of us are aware that most adults need eight to nine hours of sleep a night in order for the chemical processes in our brains and bodies to function correctly, but we don't always make sleep a priority. To accomplish a decent night's sleep there are some tips to follow. First, go to bed and get up at approximately the same time so that your body gets in a rhythm. Second, only use the bed for sleep and sex. Do not read, watch TV, or do other activities in bed. Screen-time before you sleep often makes falling asleep harder. You want to train your mind to prepare for sleep when you get in bed. Third, do not drink caffeine for several hours prior to bed time. Fourth, do not eat a heavy meal for several hours prior to bed time. Fifth, do not exercise for several hours prior to bed time. Sixth, sleep in a dark, cool room.

Shortages of certain vitamins and minerals can cause sleep disruptions. Recommendations for remedying these issues are outside the scope of this book, but if you experience chronic sleep problems it would be worth a visit to a functional medicine doctor. These doctors specialize in utilizing nutrition to heal imbalances underlying many physical conditions such as insomnia. Most Americans don't eat enough vegetables and are deficient in minerals like magnesium and potassium which are vital to getting proper sleep. A functional medicine doctor can use blood work to identify nutritional deficiencies and help you restore balance to your body.

Sleep is very important for your mental health. You cannot function effectively if you are not physically and mentally rested. Due to your depression and/or anxiety, it may be difficult for you to sleep throughout the night. You may need to engage in the activities suggested in this book and feel better before you are able to sleep in a healthy way. Even if this is true, we encourage you to begin practicing healthy sleep habits so that when you do feel better, you will quickly be able to get into a healthy sleep pattern.

Connection

Human beings need connection. If we are serious about getting our stress levels under control in order to decrease anxiety and depression, we have to consider our need for connection. Connection to nature is one well-researched way to decrease cortisol in the body. Berto, in an article called *"The Role of Nature in Coping with Stress"* says, "Just walking for a few minutes in a natural setting significantly lowers your stress level." Get outside! Find a walking trail. Walk the dog. Take a hike on the weekend. Nature really is good medicine when it comes to stress.

Healthy connection to other humans is equally important when it comes to lowering stress and improving depression. According to an article in Psychology Today called *"The Dangers of Loneliness,"* people who are isolated just aren't as happy.

Our culture doesn't promote community easily. People move in and out, and it can be hard to find a group of people you feel comfortable with. You have to push beyond the uncomfortable and reach out. Try a place of worship, a volunteer activity, or a civic organization. Take a class, or join a singles group. Take a deep breath, and go where other people are. Feeling connected is one step closer to feeling healthy.

Alison's Experience Recognizing and Managing Stress

The process of identifying and mitigating the stressors in my life paid dividends when it came to dealing with anxiety and depression for me. I felt guilty about being stressed as a stay-at-home-mom with a flexible schedule and no significant health or money problems. I'd had a decent childhood and no big traumas. How could I be stressed?

At first, I dismissed stress as playing a role in my depression or anxiety. However, as I learned to check in with my body, I found a different story. My low back hurt when I worked too hard. My shoulder ached when my kids fought. My heart rate increased when I entered confrontational situations. It struck me as a weakness, but I realized I experienced pretty strong symptoms from normal, everyday stressors. Most of the time, although I was unaware of it for years, I reacted like one giant, raw-nerve ending to situations and people around me. I didn't know why, but I just felt angry a lot of the time, not mildly ticked off but full of a black, hot energy that overtook my body. Small things, like finding out someone said something about me, sent me reeling. Big things, like break-ups, sent me into the pits of despair.

Once I recognized this pattern, I began to be able to address it. I took up yoga and walking the dog because I really hate any kind of jumping around exercise. I was skeptical of mindfulness and meditation. I thought it was a huge waste of time, but desperation will make you try anything. I remember something clicked for me when I heard somewhere, "You are not your thoughts. You have your thoughts. They are in you, but they are not you. And, a thought can be changed." I didn't know if I had thoughts so much as overwhelming feelings, but the only hope for changing the reaction to thoughts and feelings that I could find was mindfulness. Then, as I read more and more about the brain imaging and science-based success of mindfulness, I decided I had nothing to lose. I started with guided meditation because there was no hope in hell for me to quiet my own thoughts. I lay there on the floor, feeling like an idiot, for five minutes at first. Five minutes felt like hours, but gradually, my time increased. Slowly, I found guided meditation teachers on YouTube who led me toward a still, quiet place inside me that I never knew existed. Slowly, even the teachers who sounded ridiculous at first, began to feel more comfortable to me.

It wasn't a dramatic change. In fact, it was so subtle that it took me a while to notice and make the connection. First, I recognized it with my kids. During instances when I would normally fly off the handle, there began to be a very palpable pause—just a second or two—where I could catch myself, and take a breath rather than ranting in made up cuss words. I began to have more fun with my kids.

There were instances when I sat in meetings that would normally cause my heart rate to go crazy, when I noticed a difference. Instead of boiling over some blow-hard who would just not shut up, I found myself counting my breaths. I began trying to send compassion to the people who drove me the craziest.

It is still hard to respond, rather than react, in arguments with my spouse. That one is still too close. I can't seem to find that second. But, I recognize the symptoms of heat in my stomach rising up to my chest, a darkness filling in behind my eyes, and increased heart rate, and *sometimes* I can walk away. That is progress. Slowly, these changes have paid off. It is hard to make time for the practices that keep me sane, but the alternative is miserable, and misery is just the reminder I need to get my priorities back in order. I strongly underestimated the effects of stress on my body and mental health. Most people do. We consider it a normal part of life. Our harried, busy schedules and worries about money, health, or family just seem like part of life to most of us. In my personal journey toward mental health, figuring out how to lower my levels of stress was the last piece of the puzzle to achieving a level of serenity I had never before experienced.

Summary

In closing, we would like to provide a summary about why stress is an important factor in helping alleviate or in exacerbating depression and anxiety.

- Stress tries to protect us.
- Many of us exist in "Full Catastrophe Living" reacting to small traumas in significant ways.
- Exercise is a good way to discharge stress from the body
- The foods we choose can increase and lower stress and cortisol
- Consistent mindfulness practice mitigates the stress response cycle
- Connection to others and meaningful communities buffers your system from stress

Stress is a part of life that we cannot control. It is part of the human condition. In some situations, we can choose behaviors and connections that mitigate the amount of stress we experience, but we cannot eliminate it completely. The piece we can control is our reaction to stress. Choose healthy foods and connections, get a regular exercise routine, and add a mindfulness practice to your daily schedule. Once you recognize and begin to manage stress, depression and anxiety often begin to dissipate.

Chapter 5
Let Food by Thy Medicine

Here is a familiar story. Over the years, during extremely low moments in her battles with mental health, Sarah sought relief from various counselors, OBGYNs, and psychiatrists. One told her that she was probably missing God, but most led her to believe, as they did, that this "condition" was simply part of her DNA. She felt particular guilt about being raised by a nice family, where she wanted for nothing. Why couldn't she just get happy? Forget happy. What about just okay? One counselor told her, "Listen, I was born with a hole in my heart. Thankfully there is great medicine to let me live a long life in spite of my unlucky genetics. You can manage your condition too."

Unlucky genetics is a common diagnosis our culture places on people with mental health problems, but this view is changing. Didn't our culture used to say the same thing about heart disease? Diabetes? Weight problems? The truth, we are finding out, is much more complicated. In a great Pop Tech Talk, Dr. Orenstein demonstrates quite clearly that we have the ability, based on our diet and lifestyle, to actually turn on good genes and turn off bad ones. Health researcher and reporter, Donna Jackson Nakazawa, demonstrates through her work that most diseases and disorders are multifactorial. Genes plus diet and lifestyle, stress load, and environment all fill our barrel until it overflows, and we present with a "condition."

Whether anxiety and depression are symptoms of a root problem or the result of faulty genes, we have to begin asking ourselves what we can do to correct the underlying issues, to lower the load in our barrels back down below the rim. We have to begin by understanding that anxiety and depression do not live in our heads. They are not just brain disorders. They are a result, in part, of a complicated biochemical interaction that takes place at the cellular level.

Alison's profession as a qualitative researcher led her down a journey to find out what and how healthy people ate. She doggedly researched how food and supplements impact mental health. The following is a summary of what she found. If you would like a more in-depth study of foods and mental health, please read Dr. Mark Hyman's *The Ultra Mind Solution*, or Dr. Kelly Brogan's *A Mind of Your Own*.

How to Eat for Happiness

I can't claim that I changed my diet with amazing will power. I did it out of desperation for my daughter, who at four developed a disturbing sensory disorder. I describe this journey in detail in *Growing the Good Life*, but in my plight to save Cecelia, she saved me. Call it a fad if you like, a modified Paleolithic diet is recommended by every single integrative physician as the basis for good mental health. You can make it as complicated as you like, but I am not a good cook. Simply stated, replacing sugar, grains, processed foods, and dairy with healthy vegetables, some meat, fruits, nuts, and seeds as the bulk of your calorie intake will reduce your inflammatory load.

Believe me, I understand. This is not the news you wanted to hear! I mourned my unhealthy food habits (and some I thought were healthy that turned out not to be like organic breakfast bars,) until a year after I began the food journey with Cecelia. I went to my annual OBGYN visit after accidentally missing a year (please don't do this), and that visit changed my attitude forever. I met with the nurse who checked me in and she read out a list of conditions I complained about over the last decade.

"Still have pretty severe PMS?"

"No, actually. It's been okay lately."

"What about migraines?"

"No. I can't remember the last one."

"Still on antidepressants?"

"No, not for a year, now."

And on and on, my answers were no, no, no! I practically leaped down the hall because it finally dawned on me. The only thing different between my last visit and this one was the food and a daily meditation practice I picked up to carry me through the rough spots.

My doctor asked, "Hey Alison, how are you?"

"I'm better than you've ever seen me!" I told him and for the first time ever, I leaped up on that white-papered table.

After five years of tweaking this system to make it achievable with busy schedules, budgets, and three children, I recommend this five-part health turn-around based on my research of dozens of women who were able to successfully get off antidepressants and on my personal experience. This is a lifestyle change, not a temporary diet, so go slow. Fully incorporate each level of change before you move onto the next. You should start to feel the effects after the first two steps, Adding-In and Replacing, within a week or two. You may decide to stop there, or keep going for more significant results.

Keep a journal and note your level of mental/physical well-being each day at the top. Give these a number from one to ten, and don't judge your number or exaggerate it. Just breathe for a few moments and ask how you feel each day. Write down exactly what being healthy would look and feel like on the first page of your journal. For example, "I will have enough energy to carry me through the afternoon. I will feel creative, energetic, and sharp. I will experience my menstrual cycle without significant irritability, cramping, or headaches."

On the second page, write down an exhaustive list of health concerns, problems, or difficulties. Just remain curious about the changes taking place in your body, they may be subtle at first. You may not notice the absence of a migraine or a panic attack until some time has passed. If you are female and are still menstruating, make special note of your menstrual cycles each month and your premenstrual symptoms.

Each day, jot down an affirmation for your health. Motivational author, Louise Hay's famous affirmation is a good one, "Every day, in every way, I'm getting better and better." Steal hers if you need to or create your own that is a bit more specific to your needs. Mine for years was, "I am healthy and peaceful." Then, write down what you did to take care of your health that day. For example, "Went to yoga. Walked the dog. Ate four cups of veggies today. Ordered water at dinner."

That's it! Focus on what you are doing right, and stay curious about the mental and physical changes taking place in your body. Let's get started.

Add-In

Before you give up anything, before your oppositional defiant brain kicks in and convinces you that gluten-free Oreos are probably Paleo-friendly, start by increasing your nutrient intake significantly. I call this Adding-In. In this phase, you will continue eating exactly as you have been eating and add in three things to your daily routine:

- Add in a green smoothie or a salad each day
- Add in daily supplements (you may want to get blood-work done by an integrative doctor to see what you need)
- Add in herbal tea

One of the highlights of my writing career came when I received an email saying that Dr. Terry Wahls, M.D. agreed to do the preface for my book, *Rethinking Women's Health*. I almost fell out of my chair when I opened it, because this woman is a giant in the integrative medical field. She effectively put her own aggressive multiple sclerosis into remission with diet and lifestyle changes that eventually became *The Wahls' Protocol*. Dr. Wahls pulled herself back from the brink, facing a zero-gravity wheelchair and dementia, and is now riding bikes and chairing a major medical research hospital unit. She epitomized the outliers I was researching for that book about women who found healing.

Dr. Wahls says that as hunters and gatherers for thousands of years, humans achieved a much higher diversity of vitamins, minerals, and nutrients than we do today. In fact, her research demonstrates that in order for our cells to function correctly we need nine cups of vegetables (in three different categories) every day. NINE! Most of us don't come anywhere close. You can move toward that number of needed nutrients by adding-in.

Add a green smoothie to your breakfast routine. My family doesn't leave the table without a greens, kefir, and frozen blueberry/banana smoothie. There are hundreds of healthy smoothie recipes out there, but I am not creative in the kitchen. I know that all the kids and my husband can stomach this one, and I can make it when I am still half asleep. I know, if we get NOTHING else healthy that day, we have at least consumed one cup of vitamin packed greens, antioxidants in the blueberries, and probiotics through the kefir.

Speaking of probiotics, if you haven't been convinced by now of the power of these invisible superheroes on health, please stop reading and watch Dr. Kelly Brogan explain why healing your gut by rebalancing your microbiome can heal your brain in the short video *From Gut to Brain and Back Again* on YouTube. The gut is called the "second brain" by physicians like Dr. Brogan for good reason. The vagus nerve carries messages from our digestive system to our brains that tell it which chemical processes to undertake. When we rebalance our microbiome by adding in powerful, but easy to find, probiotic supplements (or if tolerated, fermented foods) we help our bodies address a key root cause of anxiety and depression. Add in a probiotic or probiotic-rich fermented food or supplement daily. Fermented foods include kombucha, a fermented tea you can buy or make, kefir, a liquid-like yogurt, and fermented vegetables like sauerkraut or Kimchi.

But these aren't the only supplements needed for decent mental health. In his book, *The Ultra Mind Solution,* Dr. Mark Hyman says that most Americans need to supplement, at least periodically, in several key areas. He recommends a quality multivitamin, fish oil for omega fatty acids, calcium/magnesium, Vitamin D4, a probiotic, and complex B vitamins. That sounds like a lot! You can get many of these from foods once you are rebalanced, but begin by adding them in to receive benefits quickly.

Finally, add in an herbal tea or infusion daily. I used to classify herbs with fairy tales, but I greatly underestimated their power. Herbs are packed with vitamins and nutrients. For example, oat straw contains high amounts of vitamin A and C, and many B vitamins including B 6, folic acid, niacin, riboflavin, and thiamine. It contains low amounts of vitamins E and K. Oat straw is rich in minerals such as calcium, chromium, iron, magnesium, phosphorus, selenium, silicon, and sodium; and contains small amounts of cobalt, manganese, potassium, tin, and zinc. Additionally, oat straw contains protein and some amino acids such as arginine, histadine, leucine, lysine, phenylalanine, and tryptophan. Wow!

I make my own blend for women's health based on my research from Mountain Rose Herbs. You can also buy quality herbal teas in the grocery store. Choose an herbal tea that decreases inflammation and increases vitamin intake. Stinging Nettle is my favorite because it is a powerhouse of vitamins and minerals. Dandelion root helps liver function, inflammation, and has been shown to decrease depression.

Replace

The next step toward rebalancing your body for good mental health is to replace some of your more harmful foods with healthy alternatives. I'm going to recommend three replacements, but start looking for others. My recommendations are:

- Replace your drink with water, herbal tea, and/or kombucha (if fermented foods are tolerated).
- Replace your lunch with a salad.
- Replace sugar with honey.

In the South, we have a sweet tea addiction. It's more like an obsession. Frankly, we consider it rude not to offer this beverage to guests at mealtime. But, sweet tea is loaded with sugar that contributes to oxidative stress and inflammation by binding with our cells, changing their structure, and interfering with their normal function. Even seemingly healthy choices like fruit juices send your glycemic index through the roof. Replacing sugary drinks with diet alternatives increases the amount of inflammatory chemicals we are throwing into our systems, and our glycemic index rises anyway because it cannot tell that the fake sugar has no calories. What got my family off of unhealthy drinks for good was finding kombucha, which is a fermented black tea that is semi-sweet, bubbly, and full of probiotics. You can buy it at most grocery stores, where it is expensive (read the label because some brands have more sugar than others), or learn to make your own. We also made it a practice to only order water at restaurants, mostly because my husband is frugal, but also because it becomes normal. Our kids don't think to ask for anything but water until we eat out with other families. You can save at least ten dollars on a family meal out if everyone simply says, "Water with lemon." In a year, if we eat out six times a month, we figure we save enough money to buy at least two airplane tickets to go somewhere great.

In our house, there is simply nothing to drink but water, almond milk, coffee, or tea. Anything else just isn't an option. Can you imagine the calories and sugar you would save in a year if you did nothing but change your drink, not to mention the chemicals, food colors, and money?

Second, replace your lunch or dinner with a salad. Make this salad the most interesting, full of flavor salad you can think of, but buy or make a healthy dressing. Replacing one meal a day with a salad goes a long way toward eliminating inflammatory foods and increasing your nutrient intake toward that nine cups a day. You now have a green smoothie, a vitamin packed herbal tea, and a salad in your meal plan.

Salads are easy. Grab a huge handful of organic greens out of the convenient boxes sold at any store. Add on a healthy protein like canned salmon or nitrate-free lunchmeat. Doctor it up with colorful veggies like sliced peppers, purple onions, olives, or carrots. You can even pre-make salads for the week in canning jars and toss them with healthy dressing like olive oil and balsamic vinegar at work.

The third replacement is sweet. Go to your farmers' market or health food store, bite the expensive bullet, and buy a great jar of honey. Now go home and throw out all the white sugar and artificial sweeteners. It takes a while to get used to the taste in baking. Half a cup of honey equals one cup of sugar. This replacement is important for two reasons. First, honey, although it causes your glycemic index to spike just like sugar, is full of beneficial properties. Honey is like liquid gold with anti-allergy, antimicrobial, anti-inflammatory, and antifungal properties found nowhere else in nature. Second, because it is so expensive, I have found that I think carefully about using it. I might cut the amount of sweetener in a recipe even more than I would if I were using cheap, white sugar. Sugar is quite simply toxic, addictive, and destructive to our bodies. Humans are designed to seek out sugar for survival. By now, we are familiar with the studies that show eliminating sugar proves more difficult than giving up heroin. Honey serves as a happy medium between health and disease.

Exchange

You should start to feel the effects of Adding-In and Replacing within a week or two. You have increased the amount of nutrients your body receives on a daily basis by adding a green smoothie, a salad, herbal tea, and supplements each day. And, you have started to significantly reduce the amount of sugar your body has to process while increasing your healthy fluids. You may choose to stop here, and your body and brain will thank you! Increased energy, weight loss, and decreased brain fog are all possible using just the first two steps. However, if you are encouraged by your results or want to see more significant results, move into the next step slowly.

Exchange means switching everyday food items for healthful alternatives, and it takes time. Exchanging healthy foods for unhealthy foods in your home can dramatically improve the quality of nutrients your body receives over time. For example, grass fed beef and eggs are loaded with vitamins D and B, which are fundamental for optimal mental health. Feedlot beef and eggs have little if any of these important vitamins.

I will list some important exchanges, but don't stop there. Every time you go to the grocery store, read the labels of your regular foods. If there are ingredients you can't pronounce, or more than five ingredients in the product, exchange that food or brand for a different one. This means paying attention. I read the labels of fourteen barbeque sauces before I found one without high fructose corn syrup. Fourteen! I read the backs of twelve fruit snack boxes before I determined it would just be cheaper and healthier to buy my kids a bag of apples. Many foods packaged as healthy are not. For example, the organic section at our grocery is full of cereals that are non-GMO, organic, and loaded with sugar. The only way to learn what is in your food is to read labels. My kids have gotten pretty good at it. I'll say, "Go find gluten-free cookies with less than eight grams of sugar and no more than five ingredients." Then I keep shopping. If they want the product, they will find it!

Here are some exchanges you can begin to make:

- Exchange the "dirty dozen" fruits and veggies for organic—these are the twelve most highly contaminated fruits and vegetables as listed by the Environmental Working Group (www.ewg.org) each year.
- Exchange your condiments for those without high fructose corn syrup, high sodium, food coloring, or unhealthy oils.
- Exchange vegetable oil for coconut oil or avocado oil.
- Read labels to find healthy soups, tomato sauce, and salad dressing.
- Choose at least one grass fed meat.
- Change your margarine for real butter.
- Exchange canned tuna (full of mercury) for canned salmon.
- Exchange chips for popcorn.
- Look at your grain purchases—breads, pasta, cereals—and find options with fewer ingredients, less preservatives, and less sugar.

Exchanging is all about reading labels. Packaging can be deceiving, especially health food packaging. You have to look at what is actually in your food. Sourcing food is also important. This is the step where you may want to learn how to grow a small vegetable garden or discover your local farmers' market. Once you start looking into what is in your food, you discover that going to the source is your safest bet.

Quality food is expensive, but so are pharmaceuticals, missed work, and doctor's visits. There are tricks to make it less costly, though. Buying half-a-share of a grass-fed cow that you store in the freezer is way more cost effective than buying the same amount of meat weekly at the store. Buying organic vegetables and fruits in season is affordable. Freeze them to use for the rest of the year. Eating in saves loads of money over a year, and it means you know exactly what quality of food is going into your body. Gardening is great for mental health and helps cut down on the cost of chemical free produce.

Eliminate

When I heard depression and anxiety described as "inflamed brain," little bells went off for me. Stop reading right now and watch Dr. Wahls Tedx Talk called *Minding Your Mitochondria*. In this talk, Dr. Wahls effectively demonstrates what our cells need to consume in order to function correctly. It also tells us what foods we need to avoid.

We know from experience that the gut-brain connection is at least a two-way street. Think about what going up on stage does to your stomach. How does a fight with your spouse impact your belly? Our brains and our guts are connected.

The stomach is called the "second brain" because it sends signals via the vagus nerve based on what it encounters. The enormous groups of nerve tissues in the gut are called the enteric nervous system. An article by John Hopkins Medicine, called *The Brain Gut Connection*, explains how irritation in the gastrointestinal system sends signals to the central nervous system that trigger mood changes. For example, physicians used to think that the high correlation between irritable bowel syndrome and mental health problems ran downstream. They thought depression and anxiety caused irritable bowel syndrome. Research now demonstrates that it is possibly the other way around.

How do we soothe an inflamed brain? How do we heal what is being called "leaky gut" so that harmful substances don't cause our guts to send an alarm signal up the vagus nerve to our brains? We have to remove the inflammatory substances we are putting in our body.

The elimination phase is for people who are really in trouble and are ready to see dramatic results. It is hard. What causes inflammation for each person is different. The only reliable way to know which foods we are sensitive to is to undertake what is called an elimination diet. You cut out all possible suspects and add them back in slowly.

The first time I tried an elimination diet I failed miserably. I detailed this debacle in *Growing the Good Life*, but here's the thing. I noticed something. It caught my attention enough to try again. Over the period of about a year, I learned a new way to eat and prepare food that avoided most of the common triggers. The following are the most common foods that people have trouble with.

- Gluten-Containing Grains
- Dairy
- Eggs
- Shellfish
- Legumes
- Food Coloring
- Sugar
- Corn
- Soy
- Coffee
- Sugar and Sweeteners
- Other intolerances that are less common like night shade vegetables, beef, or pork

You may only be sensitive to one or two of these foods. It is important to remember that intolerance is not an allergy. Food intolerances involve the digestive system. Food allergies involve the immune system. Healing our guts to heal our brains is what we are after.

People often notice increased energy and decreased brain fog within a week. Moodiness and irritability decrease over time. For women, noticing your pre- and menstrual symptoms is a good gauge of progress. The key is to keep a journal.

I recommend following one of the following protocols:
- *Clean Gut,* by Dr. Alejandro Junger, M.D.
- Whole 30

- *The Ultra Mind Solution,* by Dr. Mark Hyman, M.D.
- *The GAPS Protocol – Gut and Psychology Syndrome,* by Dr. Natasha Campbell-McBride, M.D.
- *The Wahls Protocol,* by Dr. Terry Wahls, M.D.

Once you figure out which foods cause you to feel unwell, begin designing a diet that eliminates them all together. This takes time. Be patient with yourself. In the first year, my goal was "two days on my good diet for every day off." It took a long time to find permanent substitutes for the foods I used regularly. For example, I tried dozens of gluten free breads before I settled on one that actually resembled bread. There is definitely a mourning process that goes into replacing the foods we love.

During the first years, I sometimes said, "Screw it!" and ate the foods on the tailgate table. Within a month, I would regret it. It became clearer and clearer that if I wanted to feel well, I had to eliminate certain foods. The trick was to find similar foods I loved and to focus on the feeling of wellbeing, rather than the sense of deprivation. I didn't want sensitivity to gluten to be the answer, but at least there *is* an answer. It isn't the whole or only answer, but for me and many other people, food is a big part.

Amino Acids, St. John's Wort, and Methylation

It is much easier to find integrative healthcare professionals than it used to be. And if you cannot find one near you, you can access almost everything online. It took a few years of research and trial and error for me to determine four things:

1. I am very sensitive to gluten and sugar.
2. I have a common MTHFR gene mutation that requires loads of vegetables and probiotics in order for my brain to function optimally.
3. My body responds well to the amino acid SAMe.
4. I had no healthy coping mechanisms for stress.

This is not the answer for everyone, which is part of the maddening thing about mental health. Every person is unique, and what your body requires is specific to your particular gene set, lifestyle, and diet. But, I challenge you to find out what your body does need. Once you support your body, the relief from anxiety and depression will come.

Methylation and the MTHFR gene is receiving a lot of attention today in integrative health communities. Methylation is a chemical process that helps rid the body of toxins and produce neurotransmitters like serotonin and dopamine. I have read estimates that between one-third and over forty percent of Americans have at least one MTHFR gene mutation—theoretically caused by the dramatic shift in our food and environmental system over the last two hundred years. This process is complicated and I didn't pay enough attention in chemistry class to explain it well. You can look it up, but if you suffer from anxiety and depression, you likely have at least one, if not two, of these gene mutations. What you need to know about this mutation is that we can alter it with our diet. Supplementing lots of green vegetables and sulfur-rich vegetables with vitamins B6, B12, and the active form of folate provide relief. Probiotics, the amino acid SAMe, and methyl donor trimethylglycine may also provide benefits.

Amino acids are essential to good mental health because they help produce neurotransmitters that regulate mood, and our typical food system doesn't provide what we need. Meat from grass fed animals is much higher in amino acids, but most American meat comes from feedlots. There are several over the counter amino acids you can try that may provide relief. 5-HTP, Tryptophan, Glutamine, GABA and SAMe are all possibilities. I recommend reading *Depression Free, Naturally,* by Joan Mathews Larson, which is the most complete work on amino acids and mood.

For natural, low-risk relief of anxiety and depression, read about St. John's Wort drops. The effects are slow and subtle, but this wonder-herb is effective. My neighbor from Germany says doctors in her country prescribe it for mood disorders over any other prescription. There are some interactions with other drugs, so do your homework. For example, St. John's Wort decreases the effectiveness of birth control. You can order the drops online or find them a local health food stores.

Fasting

There are several routes to recovery from anxiety and depression. The purpose of this book is to present all the effective tools we know about so that you can choose the right path for yourself. Water fasting has been shown to reset levels of depression and anxiety, with significant improvement for schizophrenics. Fasting is not starving. The mechanisms for relief aren't definitive, but are possibly linked to a rest for the digestive system that helps seal and heal the gut lining. Once the gut is healed, inflammatory substances can no longer leak through and into the bloodstream where they wreak havoc on the body. Another reason water fasting may help relieve symptoms is because it activates the parasympathetic nervous system in the same way mediation, acupuncture, and other holistic modalities do.

While we don't fully understand exactly how it works, the fact that fasting serves as a protective mechanism for our bodies may be why it is an integral part of almost every major religion in some form. In an article called "Fasting for Mental Health: Does it Work?" the author quoted a study by Michaelson et. al. in 2009 that said, "therapeutic fasting alleviates depression symptoms and improves anxiety scores in eighty percent of chronic pain patients after just a few days." Water fasting for more than three days should be supervised by a physician, and the long-term results appear to be unclear. But, perhaps it could be used as an immediate relief while you learn other methods of alleviating persistent mood problems.

Conclusions

Could I eat what I want and be mentally well? Maybe. But, for me, it would take much more effort in the other lenses that are discussed in this book. I could retrain my brain around my moodiness or even rage with enough practice even if I didn't change my diet. But, it would be like running uphill with a refrigerator on my back. When I start with functioning cells, I can get the rest to fall into place more easily. When my brain does not feel inflamed or on fire, I can make better decisions about the rest of my mental health.

Here is a summary of the nutrition techniques discussed in this chapter:

- Add in foods that support mental health—more vegetables and fruits that provide micronutrients and vitamins the body needs for good mental health.
- Replace foods that increase inflammation with foods that feed your brain and body
- Exchange foods you may be sensitive for comparable alternatives
- Eliminate foods that cause you to feel unwell
- Look into supplements, vitamins, and alternative treatments like amino acids and St. John's Wort that produce protective neurotransmitters
- Research fasting as a means for relief

For you, starting with brain training, relieving stress, or releasing trauma may be more effective. Again, any angle you choose creates change, and change ripples out. Nutrition may not be the right path for you. If it isn't, do not beat yourself up. Address one of the other lenses in this book and get started. If it is for you, find a health care provider to help guide you if you can. I do believe that when you take care of the whole body, the parts fall into place over time. Look at this endeavor as a grand journey in getting to know yourself. You will begin to see the connections between your behaviors, choices, and mood, which is empowering because it means you are not simply a slave to your mental health. You have a choice. You can impact change in your own body, and that is powerful!

Chapter 6
Feeling our Feelings

One of the greatest contributors to problems with depression and anxiety is a resistance to the very simple act of feeling our own feelings. Feeling our feelings is not the same as thinking about our feelings, analyzing their root causes and devastating effects, venting them to a sympathetic friend, therapist, or spiritual advisor, or taking them out on our nearest and dearest loved ones. Feeling our feelings is about quietly sitting with and carefully attending to the actual physical sensations of the emotions that live in our bodies.

It sounds very simple—sit with your feelings—but in reality, this is one of the very most difficult things for most of us to do. Why is this so difficult? As Raphael Cushnir explains it in his book *The One Thing Holding You Back*, it has to do with the three-stage evolution of our brain. There is an ancient reptilian aspect, a more recently evolved mammalian innovation, and the newest development which is uniquely human. Each of these parts of the brain plays a different role when it comes to feeling—or not feeling—our emotions.

The oldest part of our brain, located at the base of the skull, developed in the reptilian stage of our evolution. Earlier in the book, we have affectionately referred to our "lizard brain," which is the part of our body that keeps us alive in dangerous situations. It is the expert that decides, based on millions of years of evolutionary experience, which survival strategy is going to serve us best in any given situation. Will it be better to run away from this angry bear, to stand and fight it, or to roll up in a ball and play dead?

In the face of danger, our conscious decision-making process goes off-line, it is too slow to be of service, and in a split-second the lizard brain has chosen a course of action. This explains why rape survivors often say afterward "I don't know why I didn't fight back." It is because the primitive brain took charge and their bodies went into freeze mode as their best chance at survival. This primitive part of the brain perceives painful emotions like fear and grief as a threat just as it would an angry bear, and it tries to cut us off from feeling the emotion to protect us from it.

Think about a time when you sustained an injury and didn't feel it until later, perhaps not until you looked down and realized you were bleeding. Just as this primitive part of our brain can shut down physical pain, it can shut down emotional pain and keep us from feeling it. This can serve us well in the short run, because if we don't feel our knee hurting, we are better able to run away from the bear. But, if we don't start feeling again, eventually it may become dangerous. If we never realize we are injured we may run on that leg until we further damage it to the point that it gives way. Just so, if we never feel our painful emotions, they build up inside us until they manifest as a mental or physical disorder.

A next big step in brain evolution came with the rise of mammals. Mammals—especially primates—have a wider and more subtle range of emotions than do reptiles. Just think about the difference in the variety of facial expressions you might see from an alligator versus those visible in a monkey. Mammals, who nurse their young, need to develop much deeper bonds with their offspring than do reptiles who are independent very soon, or even immediately after, emerging from their eggs. Emotions seem to me to be intricately linked with the evolution of this mammalian bonding process. Neurons in our brain, called mirror neurons, actually enable us to feel in our own body the emotion we see on the face of another, thereby creating an emotional bond between us.

In mammals, emotions like excitement, playfulness, anger, fear, and tenderness seem to easily come and go in response to daily experiences. The emotion seems fully felt and is easily released when an experience is complete. This cycle of fully feeling something in the moment and then moving from that feeling into the next experience is part of the emotional health of an animal and is easily visible in both wild and domesticated animals. I have two kittens who are four months old, and I witness this phenomenon every day as one minute, they are wrestling and biting each other with ears pulled back, teeth bared, and eyes blazing, and the next, they are cuddled up together grooming each other and looking supremely content and at ease. (Interestingly, and not coincidentally, the animals living in captivity and in close proximity with humans seem much more prone to suffer from the kinds of neurosis and malaise that plague humans than do animals in the wild.) Imagine having an argument with your loved one where harsh words were exchanged and tempers flared. Could you so quickly let go of anger and find yourself affectionately doting on them as the kittens do? Letting go of emotions is much more challenging for humans, and this is because of the most recent evolutionary development of our brains.

Early humans experienced intense development of the brain's frontal lobe, or neocortex, and this seems to be largely responsible for what makes us unique in the animal world. This area of the brain wants to think about, analyze, understand, explain, and evaluate every aspect of our human experience. It makes comparisons and passes judgments. It is capable of self-consciousness, it sees problems and likes to solve them, and it hates to feel as if anything is outside its range of control. To this human part of our brain, emotions need to be categorized as right or wrong, good or bad, healthy or unhealthy, etc. They seem like a problem to be solved, something out of control that needs to be handled, managed, and dispensed with as soon as possible. The last thing this part of the brain thinks we should do with a feeling is feel it, yet our human brain is also quite prone to holding onto and cherishing difficult emotions by running over and over in our minds the justifications for them and their painful consequences in our lives. This is quite different from feeling our feelings, and in fact, it drives our pain deeper and deeper into our bodies.

From these descriptions, you can see that the emotional part of our brain is outnumbered, two to one. Neither the lizard brain nor the human brain wants anything to do with the needs of the mammalian brain to feel emotion. When we ought to let emotions move through our bodies like music reverberates in the strings of an instrument, instead we try to "stuff it down" or "figure it out." These two strategies may work in the short run, but they take a terrible toll on our bodies.

The reason for this is that emotions change the chemistry in our bodies. The emotions that our human brain perceives as "negative"—anger, fear, and sadness in all their varieties—have chemical signatures that elevate the stress hormones in our bodies. In order for this chemistry to return to a neutral state, the feelings must be discharged through the act of feeling them. When our lizard brain and/or our human brain prevent the feeling of emotion, our chemistry gets stuck in stress mode, wreaking all the havoc that stress will wreak on our physical and mental health by causing a myriad of problems such as heart disease, migraines, cancer, fibromyalgia, and other autoimmune disorders as well as our old companions which are the topic of this book: depression and anxiety. (See the chapter on stress.)

Clearly it is crucial to our well-being to learn how to fully experience our emotions, but that leads us to an important question: how do you feel a feeling? We would like to give you some guidance on how to do this hard but vital work. Here is what

Lynn has learned and what she is still practicing in her personal life and teaching to clients in counseling.

Lynn's Tips on Sitting with Emotion

We must sit mindfully with our emotions, experiencing them as physical sensations, witnessing with curiosity and loving kindness their manifestations in our physical bodies, without judging, analyzing, or trying to control them. It is surprising how something that sounds so simple and so gentle can be so utterly terrifying. However, I find, time and time again, in my life and in the lives of my clients that's what it is. We don't realize we are terrified, but so much of our busy rushing from here to there; our escape into food, drugs, alcohol, and binge watching; our blame of others; and our efforts to change them stem from our terror of simply sitting quietly and allowing our feelings to rise to the surface of our awareness.

Feeling our feelings is scary because they seem overwhelming, out of control, painful. It often helps to find a companion who will sit with you as you feel. With all my years of meditation and counselor training, my emotions still scare me. Sitting with my meditation teacher beside me, I can go into dark corners that I am rarely brave enough to face by myself. I highly recommend finding a counselor to sit with you while you learn to feel your feelings. Some people are lucky enough to have a friend or family member, or spiritual teacher like mine, who can sit with feelings, but often we need to seek professional help. I have come to believe that this is one of the most important qualities to look for in a counselor. Can they stay present with your pain, just sitting there with you in it and allowing you to feel it without turning to problem-solving or analysis to help you escape from it? Whether with a companion or alone, these are some steps to take to help you learn to feel.

Mindfully Noting Physical Sensations

Emotions begin as physical sensations that we interpret and label. We feel fluttering or nausea in our belly, and we call it "anxiety." We feel our heartrate increase and our face redden, and we call it "anger." Often, we aren't really even aware of the sensation itself. The labeling happens so quickly, and once we have a name for what is going on, our neocortex usually has a story at the ready to justify this feeling or to try to talk us out of it. The anxiety is because we are afraid we're going to get fired, the anger is because our spouse forgot to do the one important task we delegated to them. Oftentimes, we get into a channel of thought that locks us into the upset. We had a thought that we might get fired and now we elaborate on it. "I've made some mistakes lately, and Joe, who just got fired, has worked here ten years. If they could fire him, they could fire me." We are angry that our spouse forgot something, and then we think, "They NEVER remember to do anything I ask. Why do I bother? They can't be counted on. I might as well just do everything myself."

We are not feeling the feeling now, we are thinking about the feeling and further scaring or angering ourselves by using our imaginations. Here is what to do when you find yourself in this situation.

Mindful Presence with Sensation

As soon as you catch yourself in a loop of thoughts about feeling, STOP!

- Check in with your body. What are your actual physical sensations at this moment?
- Instead of labeling the emotion, label the physical sensations. (Tingling in my hands, heat in my face, a knot in my stomach). Try to use neutral, vividly descriptive language that doesn't imply a negative quality to the sensation—instead of "pain in my head" try "a dull, throbbing near my temple."

- Now, sit with this feeling, and just let yourself feel it even if it is very uncomfortable.
- If you would like to, you can rate the level of its intensity on a scale of 1 to 10, but then go back to feeling.
- Now imagine you could send your breath to surround this area of sensation. Next time you breathe in, wrap air around the sensation as if you were gently swaddling it in a blanket of breath or, as Raphael Cushnir recommends, fill it with air as if it were a balloon and then on the exhale imagine the balloon deflating. Notice what happens.
- It is important to approach this with simple curiosity. You are not trying to change the sensation with your breath, you are providing your breath as a companion to the sensation and noting with curiosity anything that happens as a result. Oftentimes, the sensation lessens in intensity and gradually dissipates, but this is not the outcome you are seeking. You are not seeking an outcome; you are simply taking the opportunity to fully feel your feeling to discover what, if anything, happens when you do that.
- Keep paying attention to your body, you may notice that a new sensation in another area of the body comes to the forefront of your awareness. Turn your attention to the new sensation, and use the same approach.
- At some point, you will have a feeling of completion with the process and you can close the session by thanking your body for its messages to you.
- The relationship with your body is like any other relationship, the more you spend time paying attention to it, the more comfortably it will communicate with you.

Success Story

Joe was a smart, sociable adolescent who had struggled with anxiety ever since early elementary school when he'd had a teacher who was a harsh disciplinarian. His mother called me at the end of her rope because his panic attacks had become so extreme that every few weeks the nurse's office was calling her to come take him out of school. In therapy, he learned to observe and label the sensations that he felt at the start of what he had previously interpreted as an oncoming panic attack. As he did so, he realized that he could simply feel the butterflies in his stomach or his shallow breathing and while they were a little uncomfortable, they were nothing he couldn't handle. Over the course of just a few weeks his panic attacks gradually lessened in intensity until they completely disappeared. He described himself as having a little nervousness before classes with his least favorite teachers and more nervousness before tests, but he said, "I think that's pretty normal." He smiled. I could see the relief in his eyes. His anxiety had so come to define him that he had never been able to think of himself as normal. Being normal felt like a huge gift, one that he was able to receive because he learned to sit with his uncomfortable sensations and to realize that he was strong enough to manage them.

In Summary

Learning to actually feel our feelings may be the hardest and most significant task in overcoming anxiety and depression. Our "lizard brain" wants to protect us from anything that is scary or that makes us feel bad. It provides all kinds of distractions (physical pain, mental pain) to dissuade us from engaging with something it perceives as dangerous. In this chapter, we wanted to provide you with tools so that you learn to sit with your feelings, rather than numbing, escaping, or diverting them.

- Mindfully note sensations and learn to separate from them. You are feeling anger, but you are not anger.
- Be mindfully present with sensations and emotions. What do they feel like physically in the body?

- Understand that feeling your feelings is the way through them. Once we learn that our feelings will not kill us, they lose their negative power and become helpful guideposts.

Feeling our emotions is difficult! Some of us hold so much guilt or pain over past behaviors, incidents, or actions that we don't want to go anywhere near them. The ironic truth is that the closer we come to these emotions, the less power they have over us. If this feels too scary to do on your own, find a counselor to help you through the process. This is not a step you can avoid if you want to be truly well. When you feel strong enough, ball up your courage and jump in. There is no past too shameful, no memory too hard, no trauma too scary that no one else has lived through, transformed from, and survived it. Show yourself some grace as you enter this transformative process.

Chapter 7
Fight, Flight, or Freeze

In this chapter, we delve a little deeper into the body's autonomic responses to traumas, and what we can do about helping our bodies deal effectively with them. Sitting with difficult emotions is hard work, but the relief on the other side can be enormous. Learning to be with uncomfortable feelings and helping them move out of the body is an important step in moving beyond anxiety and depression.

When we are faced with danger, whether it is a physical danger like an abusive father or an automobile swerving out of its lane toward us, or a psychological danger like a critical mother or an irritated spouse, our body kicks into high gear. We are assessing the danger, and the "lizard brain" is deciding which one of three strategies will be most effective to respond to the danger in this situation: fighting, fleeing, or freezing, just as a wild animal would do when faced with an oncoming predator.

Animals will go through a series of physical steps first to assess danger and then to respond to it. At a sudden noise, a rabbit will move its ears, sniff the air, look around to locate the source of the noise, and attempt to identify it. A rabbit might recognize the sound or smell of a coyote. If the predator is far away, the rabbit will run off before it can get caught. If it is close by, the rabbit will freeze hoping the coyote does not notice it. If, before it can move, the predator is upon it, the rabbit may wildly kick its strong legs to loosen the predator's grip, and if it is successful, run away to safety. If it can't get free, it may suddenly go limp; if the coyote mistakes the rabbit for dead, it will often drag the rabbit home to consume it in safety, offering the rabbit one more chance to escape when the predator drops it on the floor of its den. If it has that last opportunity to run, and it makes it home to its own warren, it will sit in silence there physically reliving the moment of the capture and then shaking all of its muscles to discharge the cortisol and adrenaline that gave it the power to escape as it did. When it finishes this process, the fear is discharged and the rabbit lopes unperturbed out its door to graze in the grassy meadow that, only a few minutes before, had been the scene of its near demise.

Animals appear to have an advantage over humans in this regard. Our "human brain" interferes with our access to the "lizard brain" and "mammal brain" whose instinctive drives give animals, like the rabbit, helpful physical strategies to deal with the biochemical activation created by exposure to a threat. As innovative trauma therapist Peter Levine points out in his book *Waking the Tiger*, animals in the wild don't get PTSD. The rabbit chased by the coyote literally shook off the chemical activation in its body and then went on quite contentedly with its rabbit life never tormented by flashbacks of that horrible moment or questions like "Why me?" or regrets such as, "If only I hadn't gone to the meadow this morning..."

Because humans, particularly those in Western, industrialized cultures, have long ago lost their instincts for specific physical strategies, we have no way to restore a neutral biochemistry to our system. Once we have been exposed to a threat we remain stuck in fight, flight, or freeze mode and find ourselves constantly agitated (fight mode), anxious (flight mode), or depressed (freeze mode). Ground-breaking therapists such as Peter Levine and Pat Ogden realized through their work with severely traumatized clients that we can incorporate the strategies that other animals use to help ourselves return our system to a calm and relaxed state after exposure to a physical and/or psychological danger. In this chapter, we want to demonstrate how to effectively allow your body to discharge negative and traumatic experiences. Lynn will use a case study to illustrate these techniques.

Somatic Experiencing Therapy

Lenora grew up in a terrifying household. Her alcoholic father could explode into an abusive rage at any moment, and he almost killed her mother a number of times. Many nights, he would creep into her bedroom and rape her. When she first came to see me, Lenora could hardly function, her body constantly in a confusing fluctuation between the sudden rage of the fight response, the panic attacks of the flight response, and the immobilizing depression of the freeze response. Lenora's body was, quite understandably, hyper-vigilant for danger at all times, never able to feel safe anywhere or with anyone.

I wondered if, in therapy, I could help Lenora recover a sense of safety so that she might be able to do something as mundane as ride a bus without having a panic attack. I decided to try a simple technique taught to me by a therapist trained in Peter Levine's groundbreaking Somatic Experiencing Therapy and to combine it with some basic mindfulness practices that are a part of Acceptance and Commitment Therapy. In this technique, we borrow a strategy from animals who carefully make a periodic visual scan of their environment in order to identify any possible threats.

I suggested that, whenever Lenora found herself sitting on the bus and feeling her anxiety rise, she should visually scan her environment and then ask herself, "What is happening right now?" After she had answered that question, she was then to reassure herself that in the present moment, she was safe.

She began to try this whenever she was in public and found herself feeling anxious. She would look around and literally tell herself what was going on around her. ("There is a man sitting in front of me listening to headphones.") She would then take note of her internal sensations and label them. (My heart is beating fast; my breath is quick and shallow.) She would acknowledge the truth of her experience in the moment. "My body doesn't feel safe," and then comfort herself, "But right now, I am safe."

Instead of sitting frozen and feeling afraid, she was actively checking for danger, paying attention to her body sensations, and affirming the fact that right now, she was safe. If she chose to, she could then change to a deeper, more relaxing belly breath that, along with her calming message "I am safe," could reassure her body that she was not presently in danger. Riding the bus, something she had to do twice a day to go to and from work, became less and less stressful, and she no longer missed work because she was too afraid of a possible panic attack to get on the bus in the morning. Due to the severe nature of her abuse, she needed many other strategies and a good deal of time to fully heal her trauma, but this simple technique continued to be an important tool for her throughout her therapy.

Deep Belly Breathing

While our "fight/flight/freeze system" is powerful, there is another, lesser known system called the "rest and digest" system that counteracts it. This is also known as the parasympathetic nervous system which is responsible for slowing the heart rate, lowering blood pressure, and stimulating the digestive process. This system creates feelings of relaxation, peace, and calm. It is controlled in part by the vagus nerve which runs down the spine and extends to all of the organs. According to Harvard Medical School, there are several things which activate this nerve. Deep belly breathing, created by moving the diaphragm, is one of them. Most of us only breathe in and out of our chests, but by breathing deeply enough that our bellies move in and out, we stimulate the vagus nerve which activates the parasympathetic nervous system.

There are many different types of breathing techniques coming from a variety of traditions claiming to be the best way to activate relaxation. My current thinking is that the key is for the breath to involve deep belly breathing so that the Vagus nerve is stimulated. Each person will find a breathing exercise that works best for them, and it may change over time. I have seen dozens of clients learn to control panic attacks with this technique alone. Experiment to find the one you like best.

Summary

Part of the human condition is experiencing trauma or stressful events. Learning to become "unstuck" so that these traumas don't continue to negatively impact our lives long after they are over is one of the greatest gifts modern science has given us. We don't have to give power to events or people who hurt us if we learn effective ways to help our bodies process these traumas. In summary:

- When you get anxious, look around your environment to see that you are safe
- Label the physical sensations in your body; it makes them less scary
- Acknowledge the truth, "My body doesn't feel safe," and then reassure yourself, "but right now I am safe."
- Stimulate the vagus nerve with belly breathing

These techniques take practice. Start in situations that are less stressful to you and move outward. Remember, you are building new experiences and pathways in the brain. This takes time and persistence, but you can be a person who thrives in the present, no matter what story your past holds.

Chapter 8
Releasing, Reprocessing, & Recovering from Trauma

Many people who suffer from anxiety and depression have experienced trauma at some point in their lives, in many cases more than once. These experiences have often been blocked from conscious memory and have never been successfully resolved. In order to release trauma, we must gain a sense of mastery over what happened, the knowledge that we survived, that we are okay. Intellectual knowledge is not enough, the message can only really get through when we experience a physical release and reprocessing of the event. A physical discharge of the survival biochemistry that gets activated when we are faced with a perceived danger (whether that danger is a physical threat or a psychological one) is the most complete way to restore our body to equilibrium. Without that equilibrium, we are vulnerable to long-term effects such as anxiety and depression.

When we experience what we perceive as a threat to our life, our system has evolved over millions of years to release the chemicals necessary to temporarily infuse us with the kind of strength that would enable us to run from a saber-tooth tiger or fight with the member of an opposing tribe. The story of a mother single-handedly lifting a car off of her trapped child or a shipwreck survivor swimming an impossible distance to shore are examples of the tremendous surge of energy that the body can marshal in its defense. If we use these chemicals to run (or swim) away or to fight, they are discharged from our body, we achieve a sense of mastery, and we are able to return to a normal physiological state. However, in modern times, it is rare that we actually have the opportunity to use these chemicals as humans historically did. We can't run away from a car accident or fight a caregiver who is much stronger than us. Instead, we have to shut down (freeze) like the opossum playing dead and wait for the danger to pass. In this case, the survival biochemistry stays activated and keeps our whole system elevated to a level that makes it seem to our body as if we are still in danger.

In order to heal, our biochemistry must return to neutral, we must feel the relaxation of knowing that the danger has passed and that we made it. This requires a release of the fight/flee/freeze chemicals that are stored in the body. Body based strategies can be so much more effective than talk therapy because they physically change the pattern that keeps telling us we are in danger even when our logical mind is telling us we're not. Peter Levine has been a pioneering therapist in the field of body-based trauma release and has developed a series of techniques for physically discharging trauma based on his observations of ways that wild animals recover after facing danger. Anyone with severe trauma can benefit from working with a therapist specifically trained in a body-based strategy such as his Somatic Experiencing Therapy, mentioned in the last chapter. Here Lynn describes one tool from Somatic Experiencing and introduces some other therapies that seem to offer similar trauma-releasing benefits.

Body-Based Activation Release

The following exercise is an example of something that a body-based therapist might do to help you discharge the fight/flee/freeze response. You may try this out with a situation that has caused you to feel some minor anxiety or upset, but please don't use it to try to process your own trauma. For that, you will need the help of a trained professional. This tool begins with mindful observance of body sensations, as did the exercise for feeling our feelings in the previous chapter.

- Check in with your body. What are your physical sensations at this moment? In your mind's eye, scan over your body and notice what sensations most strongly pull your attention.
- Label the physical sensations. (numbness all over, a feeling like a fist squeezing my heart, etc.). Try to use vividly descriptive language and avoid vague, general words like "pain" that convey a negative judgment of the sensation.
- Now, sit with this feeling and just let yourself feel it, even if it is very uncomfortable.
- Now, try adding some small, slow movement of your fingers or toes (choose the one nearest to the most noticeable sensation—if your legs are heavy like lead, wiggle your toes, if your chest feels tight, wiggle your fingers. Go so slowly that you are able to feel and track the sensation of the movement of your fingers or toes.
- Breathe, and notice what, if anything, happens to the sensation that had drawn your attention initially.
- Toggle back and forth in your awareness between the original sensation and the sensations of moving your fingers or toes.
- As you do this, you may notice a tingling occur in your body, a welling up of tears, or a sense of relaxing. If so, just allow this to happen and mindfully observe it. If you don't feel a shift, that is okay.
- When you feel complete with the experience, take a few deep breaths and slowly open your eyes.

EMDR

One of the most recent therapies for moving trauma out of the body is known as EMDR, or Eye Movement Desensitization and Reprocessing. In theory, EMDR helps participants process traumatic events or experiences so that they are brought to a resolution, rather than continually replaying in the body. The therapy works by alternately accessing the right and then the left side of the brain through external stimulation such as watching the therapist's finger move from left to right before their eyes, listening to headphones with a sound going back and forth between the left and right ear, or feeling a pulse in their right and then their left hand from a device they hold. As this stimulation occurs, the therapist helps the client process the traumatic events, gradually bringing the client out of the traumatized state and back to a state of feeling calm and resourced. Successful treatment with EMDR therapy relieves distress from unresolved memories and decreases physiological arousal brought on by these memories.

People are often able to let go of the "loop" they experience again and again. Once the memory has been reprocessed, it no longer holds the emotional charge that caused it to be so painful. According to the EMDR Institute, healing from trauma does not take years of psychotherapy. "The brain's information processing system naturally moves toward mental health. If the system is blocked or imbalanced by the impact of a disturbing event, the emotional wound festers and can cause intense suffering. Once the block is removed, healing resumes. Using the detailed protocols and procedures learned in EMDR therapy training sessions, clinicians help clients activate their natural healing processes.

You can find a local counselor certified in EMDR by searching on the EMDR Institute website. You can also Google EMDR and your state or city name to find certified practitioners.

Soul Retrieval

As the scientific understanding of trauma increases, it is fascinating to see how the practices of indigenous cultures often show a deep understanding of what takes place in trauma and what is necessary to heal from it. Sandra Ingerman is a licensed marriage and family therapist who discovered "soul retrieval" as a shamanic practice that could be combined with psychology to explain the "soul" leaving the body during trauma. In psychology, we call this dissociation. From a shamanic perspective, soul loss is a common cause of illness, depression, anxiety, or addiction.

In this practice, an experienced person can "retrieve" parts of a fragmented soul. Practitioner Annie Fuller writes:

> Dissociation and soul loss are themes for the majority of my clients, whether they're physically ill or emotionally suffering. Over the past twenty years I've seen shamanic soul retrieval greatly enhance the lives of countless numbers of people, myself included. We must all come home to ourselves. How else can we live in the present moment? The here and now—no longer triggered and living out of past traumas and wounds. Free.

While this method may seem superstitious or silly in our modern culture, people who have suspended their doubts appear to experience a major relief in symptoms. We offer this as another tool that you might explore to heal depression and anxiety by healing trauma. If you seek out a practitioner, please be sure that they are properly trained and qualified to lead you through such an experience. Visit www.shamanicteachers.com to find a practitioner who is certified by Sandra Ingerman, a respected expert in this field.

Success Story with Anxiety

Arthur was a thirty-year-old computer programmer who struggled with social anxiety. He found it especially difficult to go into unknown situations such as parties or work meetings where there were people who he did not know and who might bring up discussion topics for which he felt unprepared. I suspected that he might have experienced a traumatic incident as a child, but he had no memory of anything that he thought could be at the root of his anxiety.

As we worked together with the activation release exercise, Arthur usually said he couldn't really feel anything, just numb. I had him describe the sensations that let him know he was numb and after a few sessions, he began to have more variety of sensation in his body. One day he came into his appointment in a state of high anxiety. His boss had called an impromptu meeting for which he'd felt unprepared. He had mostly stayed quiet and survived the meeting, but he had not been able to calm down since.

We began the activation release exercise, and he described gripping pain in his right shoulder and a cold, sinking feeling in his body. I asked him to wiggle his fingers very slowly, feeling each sensation as he did so, and after a few moments he said, "Wow, I had totally forgotten that."

He then described to me an incident from his childhood when he had visited Sunday school at a friend's church. The teacher was having trouble keeping the group focused on their Bible study and getting more and more exasperated every minute. When she got up for a moment and turned her back, one of the children threw a wad of paper at her. She wheeled around, grabbed Arthur by the shoulder and dragged him into the hallway. She pushed him to the floor and hissed, "Sit!" swept back into the classroom and slammed the door.

Together we walked step by step through this memory. As he mindfully described his sensations, and the reactions he had at the time, he gently wiggled his fingers. He remembered feelings of anger at the injustice of being punished for something he didn't do. His face burned, and he clutched his hands together in a fist. Seeing that his body was having a fight response, I encouraged him to mindfully allow the movement he felt inclined to make by slowly opening and closing his fingers, feeling each sensation of the movement as he did so. These slow and mindful movements released the chemicals from his muscles that told him he was in danger. Suddenly, something shifted, some tears flowed, and he felt a profound change in his body. He was okay. That was years ago. That teacher had no power over him. She seemed pathetic. He opened his eyes and smiled.

I saw him twice more after that, but there was little to talk about. He was still introverted and a little daunted by social and work situations, but they didn't instill the panic in him that they once had. He had achieved mastery over the traumatic situation and resolved the unconscious conflict that he had experienced every time he went into an unknown situation. He couldn't believe the shift that such a seemingly simple exercise had created in him.

Success Story with Depression

Marie came to me as a young adult. After years and years of abuse and neglect by her parents, she had trauma after trauma layered one on top of another. She had been a high-functioning high school and college student. Although she was consciously aware of what had happened to her—she remembered vividly many of the abuse incidents and could easily be triggered by certain reminders of her mother or father—she had managed to compartmentalize these memories and had channeled all her fight or flight energy into her studies.

She was a driven, straight-A student who graduated with honors at the top of her class. She got a great job and started in the career she knew was right for her. Everything seemed to be going well, but suddenly, she hit a wall. She began procrastinating on projects and hiding out from co-workers when they wanted to talk with her. She experienced intolerable anxiety any time she had to make a presentation to a group or travel to a conference. She had never trusted people enough to make many friends, but now she completely withdrew from social contacts.

Alone at home in the evenings she became so depressed she could hardly function. She no longer made meals or cleaned house. Once an avid crafter who always had a sewing or crochet project going, she could do nothing now beyond watch television. She did this late into the night, binge watching one program after another, often staying up until the wee hours of the morning. Her insomnia became intense—even if she managed to turn the tv off and get in bed, she couldn't fall asleep. After a poor score on her annual review, she came to me in tears, terrified she was going to lose her job, the one thing she'd focused on to keep her going all these years.

She came to therapy knowing that she needed to address the memories, and she approached it just as she always had her schoolwork—seriously. Therapy for this level of trauma takes more time, support from a trained therapist, and a brave participant. Marie was up for the challenge and insisted on working through her childhood memories piece by painful piece. Gradually over the course of her therapy, we processed the memories of her terrifying father and neglectful mother, each time utilizing the small, mindful body movements that mimicked the movements her body would have made in order to fight or run away from her abuse if she could have done so. As she breathed and felt her body—or the dissociation from her body that had occurred at the time—she gradually restored her sense of safety and mastery. She still marvels at the way the memories, whose content has not changed, have a whole different feeling to her after this work. The images are there, but they hold no charge, no power, no grip on her emotions anymore.

Over the course of her therapy she experienced periods of renewed productivity and hopefulness alternating with periods of a return to the frozenness and depression, but each time she dipped down into the despair, it was a little less intense and shorter lived. Gradually, she came to feel capable of trusting others, letting down the hyper-vigilance she had always felt, relaxing, and even feeling joy in her body. The trauma lost its place as the defining feature of her life. Instead, it was something terrible that had happened to her that she had not only survived, but had triumphed over.

Summary

Trauma release therapies appear to work quickly, and the results seem to last. Clients often describe themselves as being very sore for the day or two after working to release trauma, as if they'd had a difficult work out at the gym. This is because for all the years since their trauma, their muscles have been tensed waiting for the opportunity to run or fight. When we release the trauma, the muscles finally let go and relax, resulting in this sore feeling. The ability to live without constant fear alleviates anxiety and depression.

In summary, there are several paths to discharging trauma:
- Understand that trauma is stored in the body
- Somatic Experiencing is a body-based therapy that helps discharge trauma from the body
- EMDR is another method of reprocessing trauma so that it no longer holds the emotional or physiological charge it once did
- "Soul retrieval" is a shamanic practice used to reconnect all the pieces of the soul that fragmented as a result of trauma

While trauma, big or small, is part of most of our lives, it does not have to continue to hold us prisoner. If you are a person who is stuck because of traumatic life events, find a practitioner to help you reprocess those events and memories so that they lose their power over your life.

Chapter 9
The Gift of the Curse

Much of this book has been dedicated to reframing what we once called "mental illness" or "mood disorders" into something more accurate, more helpful. We have asserted that anxiety and depressions are symptoms of a larger imbalance, whether physical, mental, or spiritual. This imbalance could be our choice in lifestyle, life-partner, career, or work patterns. It could be an imbalance in thought patterns that formed long ago, or an imbalance in the way we treat our bodies with food and exercise. It could be an imbalance in nutrients, amino acids, or vitamins. It could be our subconscious trying to distract us from "unacceptable" or painful feelings, or it could be the result of a trauma or series of events we perceived as traumatic. While it was not our choice to create these imbalances, we can choose to look for ways to rebalance our lives and our health.

We have reframed anxiety and depression as an alarm system designed to alert us to an underlying condition or a past trauma we need to address. This alarm system will not let up until it has our attention. We have a choice. We can continue to numb, fight, flee, or roll over and play dead, or we can get on with the business of healing.

We want to suggest one more reframing of anxiety and depression. We believe, through our collective work and research, that the very thing you call an albatross may also be your greatest gift. Writer Ina Hughes once said, "There are two kinds of people in the world. Those who have looked into the abyss and those who have not." There is a depth of character, a reserve of empathy, and a willingness to create cultural change that come from having "looked into the abyss" if you have the courage to move through pain, not around it, to healing. We suggest that the very courageous act of facing your "dark night of the soul" or your "demons" makes you into something more than you once were, someone stronger, more compassionate, and more willing to live an authentic, purposeful life.

In fact, entire shamanic cultures view mental health disorders differently than our pathology-based-approach. In an article entitled *A Shaman's View of Mental Illness* the author says, "Dr. Somé proposes that what we call depression, bi-polar, psychosis and schizophrenia may perhaps be a remarkable transformation in consciousness and an inevitable step towards human development." What would it do to our experience to see it as an important passage in spiritual or emotional development?

In this chapter, Alison will describe her personal journey from seeing depression as an enemy to understanding it as a gift. We invite you to undertake this journey toward healing and whole living.

From Curse to Gift

I want to end my piece of this book by suggesting something I never would have believed ten years ago. I want to suggest that your mental health albatross may be your greatest gift. Our shadow sides are often the flip sides of our best selves, and you cannot have light without dark or day without night. Death is the reason we treasure life. These opposites cannot exist alone, but live in a tension that pulls us toward growth.

For years I longed to be "normal." I jealously watched people who seemed to worry about what to wear in the morning.

I wanted shallow, manageable thoughts and dulled feelings. But, there were gifts even then. There were gifts in seeing the world through empathetic eyes—which led me to my calling as a teacher for the most underdog of children. There were gifts in the bruised, tender feelings and depths of experience that I knew were rare—broken hearts carry beauty. There were also moments of ecstasy that I knew few people experienced—speeding in a cab through the dark, city lights of Mexico, chasing a sunset to the Pacific Ocean, screaming at the dawn from the top of a mountain.

These were not enough, of course, because the darkness bore more unbearable power and always lasted longer. It wasn't until I gathered my courage to move through the depression, instead of around or through some dulled version of it, that I realized the truest gifts. I could have chosen to use the crutches I'd gathered around me for the rest of my life. White wine and antidepressants do have their place! But, this was a half-life.

Not all periods in your life are good times for change. You have to wait for the right moment, like timing a leap onto a moving train. I had heard enough compelling stories about rewiring the brain, the impact of supporting the body with food, decreasing stress and inflammation in the body, and moving emotions through and out of the body, that I decided it was worth a try to live fully. These are the cracks that create space for change. The moments when we fling ourselves gracelessly into the lifeboat because we know our ship is sunk.

I began my own great odyssey, the adventure of a lifetime, to learn to live with myself un-numbed. My husband was doubtful—scared, in fact. I don't blame him. He had witnessed several of my attempts to go without medication. I took a last breath and dove in with my new tools, and I sunk like a bowling ball in a swimming pool.

I quickly began drowning, the whole world lost color, and my perception of everything was bleak, hopeless, and angry. But, this time, something was different. I said my prayer, "trust." I kept eating well, taking the supplements and amino acids that I knew helped support the nervous system and produced the needed chemical reactions. I surrounded myself with people who supported me, and stayed under the watchful eye of my husband. I faithfully did a fifteen-minute guided meditation every day. I went to yoga, walked the dog, and prayed. I took it easy on myself, got my toenails done, and read books about people who had crossed through. I held on and breathed on the floor in my closet until my heart rate returned to normal.

Slowly, I began to emerge. I rubbed the dirt out of my eyes and looked around, and what I found blew my best imagined outcome out of the water. I had survived! Reborn with the knowledge that this thing could not kill me. Bathed in the truth that I had the tools to make it, and that those tools would carry me.

It is not that the depression and anxiety don't come anymore. It is that when they do, I know my body is telling me something I need to hear—slow down, breathe, quit eating so much junk, define your boundaries, line up your actions with your values, and stop taking on tasks that are not meant for you.

There are dark periods, still. I have changed the way I look at these for the most part. They are usually periods where I need to rest, to learn, to cocoon, or to release something. Sometimes it takes a while to figure out what they are trying to teach me, but eventually, if I stick with it, the lesson always appears. I trust that I will come out the other side stronger, wiser, and more able to help others.

Last spring, I started to dive. My body was betraying me, I thought, with an autoimmune flare that left me covered in miserable hives for months. I started to numb. I ran for the meds the doctors suggested but had no relief. I returned to an old behavior of using my condition as an excuse to treat my family badly. I started to feel awfully sorry for myself. And then, my husband woke me up by holding up an old mirror. I saw myself as I had been before my odyssey.

I had a choice. I had the tools. I started to dig. What I found was ancient anger and full-on stress. I knew what to do with these emotions and started the work. At first, I protested, "But I've already dealt with this!"

I heard God suppress a giggle.

I started writing down what caused this rage every night before I went to bed—everything from the injustice of poverty that I witnessed daily in my work at a community center, to my kids' refusing to drink their green smoothies, to old wounds I thought long dead poured out night after night. I also started with a gratitude list to refocus my brain. I cleaned up my diet—again. And, I came through just in time to recognize myself in one of my children, who will have to come through this jagged path as well. *This* is the biggest gift. This is the generational impact that facing and embracing your demons can present. My child will not have to walk through the darkness alone.

A better life is possible. It isn't very American to be uncomfortable, but maybe it needs to be. Maybe learning to push through the discomfort is the thing we are missing at this point in our history. Maybe pushing through, or at least sitting with discomfort, is the only way to really live.

In Summary

We believe you can learn the tools to heal from anxiety and depression and to cope with them effectively when they reappear in your life. Here are our suggestions:

- Reframe the way you view anxiety and depression. Ask, "What are they trying to tell me?"
- Choose an avenue to begin addressing this wake-up call: mentally (cognitive training techniques), physically (nutrition, exercise, diet, supplements), spiritually (prayer, meditation, affirmations), or by releasing trauma (body-based activation therapies, EMDR, soul retrieval)

- Find the appropriate support—physicians and trained practitioners
- Put your chosen method(s) to work consistently in your life
- Learn to be uncomfortable as you heal—facing your "demons" is hard, but the only way out is through
- Pass it on—use your gift to help others

If you take these steps and trust that you can be well, we believe you will be. This path takes courage and persistence, but it is the path to a whole, authentic, purposeful life. It is our hope that you achieve a life that is full enough to share with others.

Chapter 10
Moving Beyond Depression and/or Anxiety

You have come to the final chapter of this book. We hope you are convinced that you have the tools to heal depression and/or anxiety. Perhaps you are still skeptical and view this as a pipe dream instead of reality. If so, it is okay. You can be uncertain and still be willing to commit yourself to trying our recommendations for a period of time to discover for yourself if this is a dream or if it is possible. In this final chapter, we want to flesh out a program for you. Do not follow this program as if it is the law. It is designed to be a model. You can use it as a pattern to design your own effective program. Play with these ideas until you find the correct combination for you.

Decide the best time of the day to meditate and exercise. These may be done one after the other, together or at completely separate times. Buddy's best meditation occurs when he is running. Alison listens to guided mediations on the floor in her living room each morning before the kids wake up. Lynn practices silent sitting mediation and deep belly breathing. We would recommend twenty minutes of meditation and thirty minutes of exercise. If you are presently not meditating or exercising, you will not be able to sustain the activity for this amount of time. Do what you can and gradually build up to these amounts. It is important that you select a time that is least likely to have interruptions and stick to this same time every day so that it becomes a habit. Make it a priority. Use the sacred writings and prayer as part of your meditation time; if you have the time, use mindful meditation in addition to the focus on sacred writings and prayer.

Spend a few minutes daily being grateful for your depression and/or anxiety. You can do this while you are getting dressed in the morning or doing some other activity that does not require your conscious attention. Rather than fighting it, ask it what it is trying to tell you and listen. Buddy worked with a lady once who had frequent headaches. He asked her to ask her current headache what it was trying to tell her and then to sit quietly and wait for an answer. In a couple of minutes, she burst into tears. When she regained her composure, she said that her headaches were telling her that she was being too hard on her teenage daughter and she needed to lighten up. Buddy asked her, when she was going to talk with her daughter, to apologize to her and commit that she would stop being so hard on her daughter. She set a definite time later that day when she would have this conversation. He asked her to make a commitment to herself that she would carry out this plan. She did and immediately she had a funny look on her face. When Buddy asked her what had just occurred, she said that her headache (which was at a seven on a ten-point scale, when they began) went away. This assured her that she had received the correct message from her headache. Buddy suggested to her that a headache coming on could remind her to loosen up. Befriend your pain; you may be amazed at what it can teach you. If you ask your pain for a message and do not receive one, don't be disturbed. Try this several times and patiently wait for a few minutes, but if no message comes, it's okay.

Use the exercises from the chapter on NLP and other strategies presented in the book. Experiment with them to discover which ones are effective for you. Practice them when you are feeling good so that you can use them when you feel discomfort. During your day, when you have a few minutes, practice one of them. The more you practice them, the more effective you will become at using them when you need them.

Be willing to experience your feelings instead of denying them. When you acknowledge them, you can work to feel better. If you deny them or fight them, they become stronger. This book is partially about learning to cooperate with your feelings instead of fighting them. As with a rip tide at the beach, you will drown if you fight the water, but if you cooperate with it, it will take you to the shore.

If you suffer from past trauma, learn to release it, or find a practitioner that can help you release it. You can learn to eliminate, or at least control it, so that it no longer rears its ugly head. It occurred in the past and you lived through it. There is no need for it to be a part of your present in a painful way. You may want to pay attention to the age you feel when you are suffering from the trauma, and then talk with that imagined version of yourself and assure them that you are living proof that they will survive. Give them encouragement.

Nutrition is important. Be sure that you are eating healthily and getting all the vitamins, minerals, and supplements that your body needs to be healthy. Your mind and body can serve you well if you take care of them and provide them with what they need to function effectively.

You may be feeling overwhelmed and saying to yourself: "There is no way I can do all that is suggested in this book." Don't try to do it all at once. Begin slowly. Do those activities that are the easiest and most enjoyable in the beginning. Be patient with yourself. If you fail one day, forgive yourself and begin again the next day. Over time, you will learn how to be a better friend to yourself, and you will come to enjoy being nice to that special person which is you!

In closing this book, we want to remind you of the exercises that have been explained in the previous chapters:

- Mindful meditation
- Exercise
- Prayer and use of sacred writings
- Listen to your pain
- Use the exercises from NLP, Mindfulness, Positive Psychology and Energy Psychology
- Manage stress effectively
- Cooperate with your pain
- Resolve past trauma
- Eat well
- Take needed supplements

We are convinced that you can be healthy. We have witnessed many clients and researched hundreds of accounts of people overcoming difficulties in their lives that seemed impossible when they began the journey. Your mind/body is wonderfully created to function effectively. We pray that this book will be helpful in your performing the miracle of living a happy, healthy life.

Sources by Chapter
In order of appearance

Preface

Brogan, Kelly. *A Mind of Your Own: The Truth About Depression and How Women Can Heal Their Bodies to Reclaim Their Lives*. Harper Collins, 2016.

Scharff, Constance. "Neuroplasticity and Addiction Recovery." Psychology Today, Sussex Publishers, 5 Feb. 2013, www.psychologytoday.com/blog/ending-addiction-good/201302/neuroplasticity-and-addiction-recovery.

Introduction

Brogan, Kelly. *A Mind of Your Own: The Truth About Depression and How Women Can Heal Their Bodies to Reclaim Their Lives*. Harper Collins, 2016.

Chapter 2

Faehndrich, Lorraine. "How To Overcome Obsessive Negative Thinking (Aka Leading Your Lizard!)." Radiant Life Design, 16 June 2017, radiantlifedesign.com.

Neff, K (2011) *Self-Compassion: Stop Beating Yourself Up and Leave Insecurity Behind*. New York: Harper Collins Publishers

Neff, Kristin. "Why Self-Compassion Trumps Self-Esteem." Greater Good, 7 May 2011, greatergood.berkeley.edu/article/item/try_selfcompassion.

Sarno, John E. *Healing Back Pain: the Mind-Body Connection. Grand Central Life & Style,* 2018.

O'Connor, Joseph, et al. *Introducing NLP: Psychological Skills for Understanding and Influencing People.* Conari Press, 2011.

Chopra, Deepak. "5 Steps to Setting Powerful Intentions." The Chopra Center, 7 Mar. 2017, chopra.com/articles/5-steps-to-setting-powerful-intentions.

Zamora, Stephanie. "The Power of Intention to Create a Business and Life You Love." Huff Post, 27 Feb. 14AD, www.huffingtonpost.com/stephenie-zamora/the-power-of-intention-to_b_4860021.html.

McKenzie, David. "How Jordan Spieth won the Masters with his Mental Game." Golf State of Mind, 13 Apr. 2013, golf-stateofmind.com/jordan-spieths-mental-game/.

Roche, Nicky. "Small Business Drivers." Cast Box, 19 Dec. 2016, castbox.fm/channel/Small-Business-Drivers-id115049?country=us.

Clary, Christopher. "Olympians Use Imagery as Mental Training." The New York Times, 22 Feb. 2014, www.nytimes.com/2014/02/23/sports/olympics/olympians-use-imagery-as-mental-training.html

Siegel, Daniel J. *The Mindful Therapist: a Clinician's Guide to Mindsight and Neural Integration.* W.W. Norton & Co., 2010.

Chapter 3

Dossey, Larry. *Prayer Is Good Medicine: How to Reap the Healing Benefits of Prayer.* HarperSanFrancisco, 1997.

Dilts, Robert/ Hallbom, Tim/ Smith, Suzi. *Beliefs: Pathways to Health and Well-Being.* Crown House Pub Ltd, 2012.

Chapter 4

Kabat-Zinn, Jon. *Full Catastrophe Living: Using the Wisdom of Your Body and Mind to Face Stress, Pain, and Illness.* Bantam Books Trade Paperbacks, 2013.

Davis, Daphne, and Jeffrey Hays. "What Are the Benefits of Mindfulness." American Psychological Association, 2012, http://www.apa.org/monitor/2012/07-08/ce-corner.aspx.

Hanh, Nhat. *The Miracle of Mindfulness: An Introduction to the Practice of Meditation.* Beacon Press, 2016.

Berto, R. "The Role of Nature in Coping with Psycho-Physiological Stress: a Literature Review on Restorative-ness." Behavioral Sciences (Basel, Switzerland), U.S. National Library of Medicine, 21 Oct. 2014, www.ncbi.nlm.nih.gov/pubmed/25431444.

Marano, Hara. "The Dangers of Loneliness." Psychology Today, 9 June 2003, www.psychologytoday.com/articles/200307/the-dangers-loneliness

Chapter 5

Nakazawa, Donna Jackson. *Childhood Disrupted: How Your Biography Becomes Your Biology, and How You Can Heal.* Atria Books, 2016.

Wahls, Terry. *Wahls Protocol.* Vermilion, 2017.

Brogan, Kelly. "From Gut to Brain and Back Again." YouTube, 17 Feb. 2014, www.youtube.com/watch?v=pKKG869s8oo.

"Healthy Body." The Brain-Gut Connection, www.hopkins-medicine.org/health/healthy_aging/healthy_body/the-brain-gut-connection.

Junger, Alejandro. *Clean Gut: the Breakthrough Plan for Eliminating the Root Cause of Disease and Revolutionizing Your Health.* HarperCollins Publishers Inc, 2015.

Larson, Joan Mathews. *Depression-Free, Naturally: 7 Weeks to Eliminating Anxiety, Despair, Fatigue and Anger from Your Life*. Wellspring/Ballantine, 2001.

Katie. "Fasting and Mental Health: Does It Work?" Mind the Science Gap, 10 Apr. 2013, www.mindthesciencegap. org/2013/04/10/fasting-for-mental-health-does-it-work/.

Chapter 6

Cushnir, Raphael. *The One Thing Holding You Back: Unleashing the Power of Emotional Connection*. HarperOne, 2008.

Levine, Peter A. *Healing Trauma: a Pioneering Program for Restoring the Wisdom of Your Body*. ReadHowYouWant, 2012.

"Relaxation Techniques: Breath Control Helps Quell Errant Stress Response." Harvard Medical School, 18 Mar. 2016, www.health.harvard.edu/mind-and-mood/relaxation-techniques-breath-control-helps-quell-errant-stress-response.

Chapter 7

Levine, Peter A. *Waking the Tiger: Healing Trauma*. North Atlantic Books, 1997.

Chapter 8

Fuller, Annie. "A Soul Retrieval Story." Full Circle Spiritual Healing, 28 Feb. 2012, fullcirclespiritualhealing. com/2012/02/28/a-soul-retrieval-story/.

Chapter 9

Logan, Kim. "A Shamans View of Mental Illness." Forever Conscious, 7 Sept. 2015, foreverconscious.com/a-shamans-view-of-mental-illness.

Recommended for Further Reading

Belief: The Pathway to Healing by Robert Dilts

Prayer Is Good Medicine, by Larry Dossey

Brief and Unusual Therapies, (e-book) by Buddy Wagner

Waking the Tiger, by Phillip Levine

The One Thing Holding You Back, by Rapheal Cushnir

The Illustrated Happiness Trap, by Russ Harris and Bev Aisbett

Childhood Disrupted, by Donna Jackson Nakazawa

Unstuck, by James S. Gordon, M.D.

A Mind of Your Own, by Kelly Brogan, M.D.

Made in the USA
Columbia, SC
10 June 2018